COSPLAY

FOR YOU

PERSONALIZED DESIGN IN CRAFTING COSTUMES

From Concept to Creation

SANIT KLAMCHANUAN

FanPoweredPRESS
IMAGINE | MAKE | BECOME

PUBLISHER
Amy Barrett-Daffin

CREATIVE DIRECTOR
Gailen Runge

SENIOR EDITOR
Roxane Cerda

COVER/BOOK DESIGNER
April Mostek

PRODUCTION COORDINATOR
Tim Manibusan

ILLUSTRATOR
Sanit Klamchanuan

PHOTOGRAPHY ASSISTANT
Gabriel Martinez

FRONT COVER PHOTOGRAPHY
by Madeleine Buddo

PHOTOGRAPHY by
Sanit Klamchanuan,
unless otherwise noted

Pages 16-17: Yothin Chankale / Shutterstock.com

Page 47: K-Smile love / Shutterstock.com

BACKGROUND TEXTURES PROVIDED BY SHUTTERSTOCK.COM:

Wongsakorn Dulyavit
Abstractor
LUMIKK555
benjamas154

Sharaf Maksumov
Automation14
Fotaro1965

Published by FanPowered Press, an imprint of C&T Publishing, Inc.,
P.O. Box 1456, Lafayette, CA 94549

Library of Congress Cataloging-in-Publication Data

Names: Klamchanuan, Sanit, 1981- author.

Title: Cosplay for you : personalized design in crafting costumes: from concept to creation / Sanit Klamchanuan.

Description: Lafayette, CA : FanPowered Press, 2022. | Summary: "Follow along with a veteran cosplayer's design process on creating original costumes from redesigns, making original designs, techniques used and breaking down costumes to components. Learn how to customize and personalize your build from inspiration to finishing touches"-- Provided by publisher.

Identifiers: LCCN 2022015451 | ISBN 9781644032404 (trade paperback) | ISBN 9781644032411 (ebook)

Subjects: LCSH: Cosplay. | Costume design.

Classification: LCC GV1201.8 .K53 2022 | DDC 792.02/6--dc23

LC record available at https://lccn.loc.gov/2022015451

Printed in the USA

10 9 8 7 6 5 4 3 2 1

COSPLAYER: Spicythaidesign
COSTUME: Warlock from *Destiny*
Photo by Chris Menges

Me in my studio
Photo by Josh Groom

ACKNOWLEDGMENTS

I just want to say thank you to everyone who has helped me to get where I am today. It has been a crazy and amazing ride, and I don't know where it will end up, but I'll keep enjoying every minute of this journey.

To all my teachers: Thank you for passing on your knowledge. I will always cherish your teachings and wisdom.

To all my family and friends: Thank you for always having my back, keeping me grounded, and always encouraging me to pursue my passion.

To Richard and the team at Wētā Workshop: I still can't believe that I work at the most wonderful place in the world. It's fantastic to be able to come to work with all of you every day and to be able to make amazing things that have changed and will always change people's lives. I look forward to many, many more years.

To all my maker friends: Without the maker community, there is no way I could be doing what I am doing today. Thank you for sharing your knowledge with the world. You all have made the world a better place by keeping the passion for making things alive.

To Mum and Brian: Thank you for all you have done for me. You have always been very supportive of every decision I have made. I hope I have made you both proud.

To Angela: Thank you for being there for me. I know it is not always fun having me work all night on my projects and putting up with all the mess I make when I am in the middle of a project. Without your support, I could not do what I do. You always push me to do what I am passionate about, and I want you to know that everything I do is for you and our little family. I larb you. (I hope I don't get in trouble with Marvel for saying this.)

CON

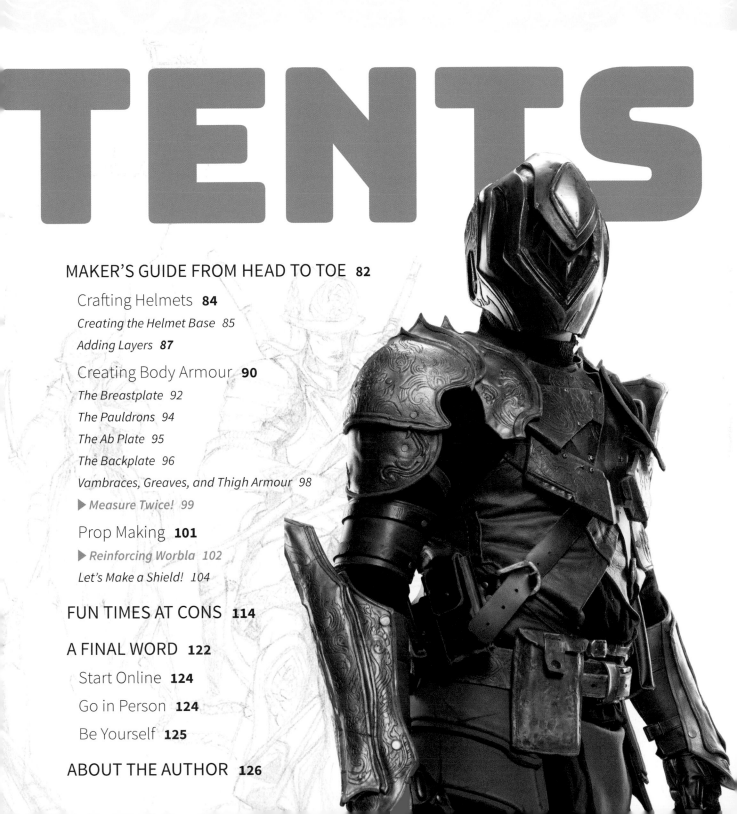

TENTS

FOREWORD

As of the writing of this foreword, I have had the great pleasure of knowing Sanit as a friend and colleague working with me at Wētā Workshop for the past seven years. If you have bought this book, it is most likely that you have been following Sanit via his various social platforms and can already appreciate what a warm, kindhearted, inspirational, and creative individual that Sanit is. Of course, it is not until you work with someone (as I and my friends at Wētā Workshop do) that you really appreciate the special qualities that someone may possess.

Sanit has intuitively understood the importance of the creative process and what it takes to step through a programme of work that leads to an end result. The need to be methodical, well planned, and organised whilst being highly inspired, inventive, and constantly curious are all components that must come together if someone is to make something impactful, successful, and of creative worth. Sanit continually demonstrates his understanding of this as he pragmatically sets about the creation of anything he does. Therefore, what he writes in this book is him sharing his philosophies around the creative journey and how he has pulled together the best of his capabilities to achieve what he does.

Sanit has never hesitated to throw himself wholeheartedly into any number of creative challenges that we may throw at him. In fact, his effort extends beyond his work hours and often into his weekend, as he desires to push further and create the best outcome for the project at hand or for his own specific hobbies and cosplay work. Whether it be producing a colouring book, a tutorial for the Wētā Cave, a costume for a conference in Switzerland, or components for a major feature film or TV series we are working on, Sanit can always be found with his hands buried in the thick of the process, excited about the opportunity and always desiring to deliver something as good as he can possibly make for the project.

His generosity of spirit and kindness of heart, coupled with his ever-growing talents, have led Sanit into a rich and rewarding career in which he now has the opportunity, through his tutorials and this book, to pass on this knowledge and in turn inspire others to follow in his footsteps.

Richard Taylor
Creative Director, Wētā Workshop

INTRO DUCTION

Hello, everyone! My name is Sanit Klamchanuan, known in the cosplay and maker world as Spicythaidesign.

My hope for this book is to inspire you to explore the artistic side of costume making and to keep you from getting stuck making the same cosplay everyone else is making. I will show you how you can add a bit of yourself to your project and create something that is special to you. Adding your favourite colour, an element from your culture, or really anything that makes the costumes and props your own will let you stand out in the crowd and, most importantly, have fun.

I enjoy putting my own twist on costumes. That can be a whole new redesign, small changes to a costume to make it more wearable, or a bit of detail incorporated into a costume to add some Thai flavour. My early years and my experiences growing up shaped how I approach my costumes. What I am about to show you is the way I like to design and make my costumes. My process works for me. Please do give it a go, but I encourage you to find your own way.

MY EARLY YEARS

Early artwork, *The Beginning*, using the Thai Naga as a metaphor for my family, beginning with my birth

I was born in a small town in Thailand and brought up in the hair salon where my mum worked as a hairdresser. As a single mum, she would often work long hours, and, being the only child, I learned to entertain myself.

Mum worked long hours, but I had my grandparents and my aunty to keep an eye on me. My grandparents were total opposites. I was the first grandson, and the only grandchild for a few years, so my grandma spoiled me. Granddad was a bit harder on me, always pushing me to do better. Even though he was hard on me, he always gave me a reason why, and now that he has passed away I especially cherish all the time we got to spend together and all the knowledge he passed on to me.

My granddad was half Chinese and a true salesman. Even into his late 80s he'd still set off on his pushbike to the market to sell bananas and veggies that he'd planted and tended on any random space he could find along the roadside. Seeing how hard my grandparents and my mum worked drove home the idea that life is hard and you have to work hard to get what you want. That is probably why I am never afraid of hard work—in fact, the opposite is true. I love it! I enjoy the challenge and the rush of a deadline, and that is when I do my best work.

Growing up, I didn't have many toys. Mum would only buy developmental toys, but sometimes I would get hand-me-down toys from friends. These were usually toys that they didn't want to play with anymore, like an action figure with a missing arm or leg, but I liked those because I got to make them new and better limbs out of modeling clay.

I pride myself on my imagination. Though I feel it is something I was born with, it was truly ignited by all the cartoons, movies, and TV shows I loved to watch. Mum told me it was like I was hypnotised, staring at the screen with eyes and mouth wide open. I soaked in everything: the story, the characters, and, of course, the action. After each show, I would sit down and draw the characters acting out my favourite moments of the show.

Check me out on the phone taking bookings! I am sure I was just pretending to call someone.

As a young child I wanted to be in the army, and then later I wanted to be a policeman, but after watching cartoons like *Dragon Ball*, *Doraemon*, and *Ultraman*, I wanted to be a cartoonist. I thought it would be a dream come true to draw all day. I created amazing characters and storylines featuring the hero saving the day. The cartoon that captured my imagination the most was called *Saint Seiya*. I loved this cartoon because of the armour! The armour had two forms. On its own, it took the shape of an animal, usually one associated with a zodiac sign. For example, the crab armour represented Cancer, but when worn by a person it would transform into body armour. Each set of armour had its own unique look, and I would often dream of owning one of these sets of armour, but I didn't have the skills to make it until now. It is still on my "want to make" list! I am sure I will make it one day.

My aunty took me to my first movie, *Superman IV*, when I was six. I remember coming home and putting a hairdresser cape on backwards, drawing an "S" on a piece of paper and sticking it onto my T-shirt, and then lying on the sofa in front of a fan pretending I was flying. I guess that counts as my first cosplay, right? I was hooked. I went to as many movies as I could. Nothing beats watching a movie on the big screen, surrounded by sound, and regretting not buying a bigger drink because your mouth is so dry from too much salty popcorn.

FROM THAILAND TO NEW ZEALAND

I moved to New Zealand when I was nine, and the transition was turbulent. I left Thailand in the middle of summer, when temperatures can be as high as 102°F (39°C), and landed in Wellington, New Zealand. If you know anything about Wellington, you know that it can be super windy! Sometimes it is so windy you have to hold on to a power pole or take the chance of getting blown away. It was a really bumpy landing, especially for my first flight, and I thought I was going to die. After surviving the landing, we travelled the twisting and narrow roads of the Wellington suburbs to reach our new home, and yes, I did throw up.

Moving to New Zealand was a new adventure, but at nine I didn't know what I was getting myself into. Not knowing much, if any, English made it even harder, and I found it very difficult to fit in. Back then, there weren't many Asians in my school, so I was placed next to Natalie, a girl who is half Thai. I always feel super sorry for her, having been forced to move from sitting next to one of her best friends to sitting next to someone she didn't know. Though our start was rocky, we got to know each other very well, and she's now one of my closest friends.

I was sometimes bullied. Being a small, skinny kid without many friends, I was picked on by the bigger, older boys. They would push me around and call me names, but because I had not yet learned a lot of English, I didn't really know what they were calling me. I turned into a very serious person. I would often take things to heart and get upset quite easily, and I couldn't take a joke because I was never sure whether my classmates were laughing with me or at me. I remember telling myself I needed to find a way to make it stop. As my English improved, I started to joke back. It must have seemed like I was easygoing and didn't take myself too seriously, but I was really afraid that if I didn't make the first joke, others would start making jokes about me.

This is when I started to lose my Thai identity. You might say, "How could you? You are Thai." Others looked at me and saw a Thai boy, but I wanted to change that image of myself and fit in. I wanted to be a Kiwi. I avoided wearing anything too Asian and even asked if we could speak English at home. I am sure that upset my mum, and, of course, she said no. I'm now happy that she refused and kept speaking to me in Thai, because if she hadn't I wouldn't know any Thai now, and that would have been a terrible loss.

One of my very early sketches, my interpretation of the Sagittarius Cloth from *Saint Seiya*

During this time, I was exposed to new cartoons like *Transformers*, *Teenage Mutant Ninja Turtles*, and *Captain Planet*. The list could go on, but the one that truly captured me was *Power Rangers*. Though the show reminded me of similar shows from Thailand, like *Kamen Rider* and *Ultraman*, *Power Rangers* was different. These characters were high school teens with problems similar to mine. Unlike me, they were able to transform into superheroes and save the day. My favourite was the Red Ranger—not because he was the leader, but because he was super confident and always kept his cool when dealing with enemies. I used to run around the playground pretending to be the Red Ranger.

COSPLAYER: Spicythaidesign

COSTUME: Red Ranger from *Power Rangers*

Me in the Red Ranger costume I made for my 40th birthday

Photo by Peter Iti of Kohika Creative

From Imagination to Reality

I'll take his opportunity to jump to 2017. I was about to fly to the United States to attend PAX West and Dragon Con. As I was saying goodbye to the workshop supervisor, I saw a picture of five heroes, one red, one blue, one black, one yellow, and one pink. I asked my supervisor, "Is that *Power Rangers*? Are we working on that?" He answered yes. I asked if I could work on the project in the costume department when I returned from my trip. I'd only been at Wētā for just over two years and was spending most of my time in the paint room and finishing department. My coworkers were aware of my cosplay hobby outside work, and when I returned from my trip I was told to report to the costume room. Working on the 2017 remake of *Power Rangers* was a dream come true. My inner 10-year-old self was jumping up and down with excitement.

My role on the project was to make all the foam prototypes for the power suits, and my first suit was the Red Ranger. I am sure my face lit up like a Christmas tree. One of the coolest parts of this job was that I was assigned the task of adding all the breakdown or battle damage for the Green Ranger. I was given a beautiful piece of green armour, and I had to destroy it. Is it bad to say that I had so much fun?

I still wanted to become a cartoonist. I figured I had watched so many cartoons it would be super cool to work on one. I was passionate about drawing and would draw as much as I could—even in my math books. I took every art class offered at Wellington College: painting, printmaking, and design. My art teachers, Tim Costeloe and Nic Scotland, were amazingly supportive. They always encouraged us to try new things and assured us that art could be a career. In my final year, I remember them staying behind after work and coming in on the weekends to make sure we completed our portfolios.

NEXT STOP ART SCHOOL

After high school, I attended Whanganui Polytech Fine Arts School (now named UCOL), a four-hour drive from Wellington. I was excited to leave home for the first time, live in a new town, and experience living with roommates.

Whanganui Polytech was the place for me. Its arts programme is well respected within New Zealand, but I think I chose it because I would get to make a printing press in my third year. In my first year, I got to try everything, including painting, printmaking, photography, sculpting, and glass blowing.

Even though I was an art student, I didn't think of myself as an artist. I was someone who enjoyed creating art, but I couldn't talk about art. I drew something because it was cool and I wanted to draw it. There were no deep and meaningful messages in my work. I can recall my first-ever painting assignment. We had to do three paintings, and they could be anything we wanted. My first painting was the Beatles, because I liked their music. The second was a painting of myself, my mum, and my stepdad, Brian, because I wanted to give it to them as a present. The third one was a painting of a shadow figure, and I guess there was a little story behind this painting.

I lived in the student flats my first year, and my bedroom was on the top floor of a three-level building. As I was walking up the stairs one evening, I turned on the light. As the light came on, a shadow rushed into my room. I thought nothing of it, but that night during dinner I told my flatmates about the shadow. They stopped eating and looked at me in shock. They told me that the last person who had stayed in my room had walked in front of a moving train and died. Just talking about it now makes my hair stand up! However, even this last painting was not a truly artistic work. When I showed my tutors my last painting, they asked me why I had chosen those colours. My answer was that they were all I had!

Receiving my arts degree from Whanganui Polytech in 2014. From left to right: Angela, me, Mum, and Brian.

For the first two years of my art programme, I struggled to come up with meaning or stories I wanted to tell in my art. I was just painting and drawing popular imagery. I even made a giant comic book for my year two end-of-year printmaking assignment.

It wasn't until I was 21 that I was finally able to put a story behind my art. You could say I found the reason I wanted to create art, and that was to celebrate my Thai heritage. In Thai culture, when a boy reaches 21 he becomes a monk for a period of time. It is a rite of passage to becoming a man. During my time as a monk, I discovered how amazing Thai culture is. I had tried so hard to be a Kiwi that I had overlooked my own culture. Being in the temple meditating and praying got me back in touch with who I am. I don't have to be just a Kiwi. I can be Thai too. I have the best of both worlds.

Some of my large comic prints

Me beginning my time as a monk. From left to right: my stepdad, my grandad, me, my uncle, my grandma, and my mum.

This piece from my first exhibition, "Kiwi Thai," depicts my mum as a Naga leaving for New Zealand, as if she were being taken away by a Garuda.

After this trip of discovery, my art went to the next level. I was no longer just copying Japanese or American comic-style drawings. I was able to integrate Thai imagery into my art and tell stories that I wanted to tell. Being a printmaking major was perfect for this! I started off small, by showing the simple idea of how everyone wears masks. When you meet someone for the first time, you often see the person they want you to see. To communicate this message, I used the imagery of someone wearing a Ramakien mask to hide their face.

My first solo exhibition, "Kiwi Thai," shared my own personal story. I used the Thai Naga to represent my story. In Thai tradition, Nagas are the serpent creatures that stand guard in front of Buddhist temple compounds or monasteries.

Using the Naga as a metaphor for my family, I started with my birth, as depicted in the artwork *The Beginning* at the beginning of this chapter (page 8). Another print was the Naga wearing a taniwha mask (Maori creature mask), pretending to be Maori, to represent how I had tried so hard to fit in. My final piece was a Naga without the mask, showing how I had come to terms with who I am. This exhibit was where I really came into my own identity.

This is a sculpture of a Thai Naga guarding the entrance to a temple.

Photo by Yothin Chankale

MY ENTRY INTO COSPLAY

At this point in my life, I worked in retail. While I was good at it, it wasn't where I wanted to stay. I had a burning desire to do something different, and the great success of my first exhibition gave me the drive to keep going, so I decided to start drawing. I had loved *The Lord of the Rings* and regretted not applying for a job at Wētā Workshop right after high school. Wētā is the company that created the armour, costumes, creatures, and much more that brought those movies to life. I watched a Thai movie called *King Naresuan*, the first Thai movie that really captured my imagination. I loved the designs of the costumes, armour, and sets. I later found out that Wētā had sent someone over to Thailand to work on this movie. *King Naresuan* and *The Lord of the Rings* inspired me to come up with a concept drawing for what would later become my Thai Armour costume.

Original pencil concept drawing for my Thai Armour

I made my first costume in December 2012 for a work Christmas party. The theme was superheroes, and I went as Judge Dredd. At this point, I had no idea how to make a costume, but I jumped on Google and YouTube to see what others had done. As I had no idea how to sew, I made the leather jacket out of duct tape, and the helmet was just masking tape over a cheap $2 shop army helmet. Looking back on it now, it's pretty bad, but I had to start somewhere, right?

COSPLAYER:
Spicythaidesign

COSTUME:
Judge Dredd from *Dredd*

Me in my first-ever costume, Judge Dredd

Human-size Binary Rifle from
Halo, made out of Styrofoam

I had so much fun making this costume that I decided to give prop making a go. I started with the material I was most comfortable with, MDF, medium-density fibreboard. I started making small knives and swords. I searched for game props on YouTube and started following Andrew Cook of DFT and his tutorials on making *Halo* guns out of closed-cell extruded polystyrene foam. His tutorials are super simple and easy to follow. Little did I know that Andrew was also based in Wellington, New Zealand. I went to a party one Friday night and chatted with this guy about building props. Then it clicked! I was talking to Andrew!

I started to take commissions, but looking back I wasn't ready yet. It was a good learning experience. I quickly discovered that I did not enjoy making things for other people or appreciate how hard and expensive it is to send anything from New Zealand.

I decided to get back into my concept drawings and discovered that White Cloud Worlds, a group of top concept artists in New Zealand, was offering conceptual drawing classes run by Paul Tobin, one of the senior designers at Wētā Workshop. To be able to learn from Paul Tobin and Warren Mahy, both world-class senior concept artists at Wētā in the White Cloud Worlds, really helped me to put my ideas into my designs, and they challenged my thinking, which pushed me to get better. But despite the great feedback that improved my drawing, I still felt that my drawings were not quite right.

It was then that I met Kim and Warren Beaton, creators of Pal Tiya, a weatherproof sculpting medium that is super strong and easy to work with. Do yourself a favour and check it out. I answered their want ad and helped out for a few days on a dragon sculpture. I showed Kim and Warren some of my drawings, and they were able to point out a few areas that wouldn't be functional as a piece of armour. My overall concept would result in armour that was too bulky, and if someone were to wear it they would be unable to move.

Inspired by my work with Kim and Warren, I made my mum a 3' x 9½' (1m x 3m) Thai Naga for her 60th birthday.

I decided that the only way to get better would be to make a costume. I'd then understand how armour works. Through my work with Pal Tiya, I met the Sowter family, who introduced me to Armageddon (not the end of the world but a New Zealand pop culture convention). The Sowters had a booth at Armageddon, and I volunteered to help in their booth. I decided to use the expo as a deadline for my first cosplay costume.

COSTUME:
Original armour with Thai aesthetic, inspired by *Halo*

Yes, I brought a Thai twist to this Halo-inspired armour.

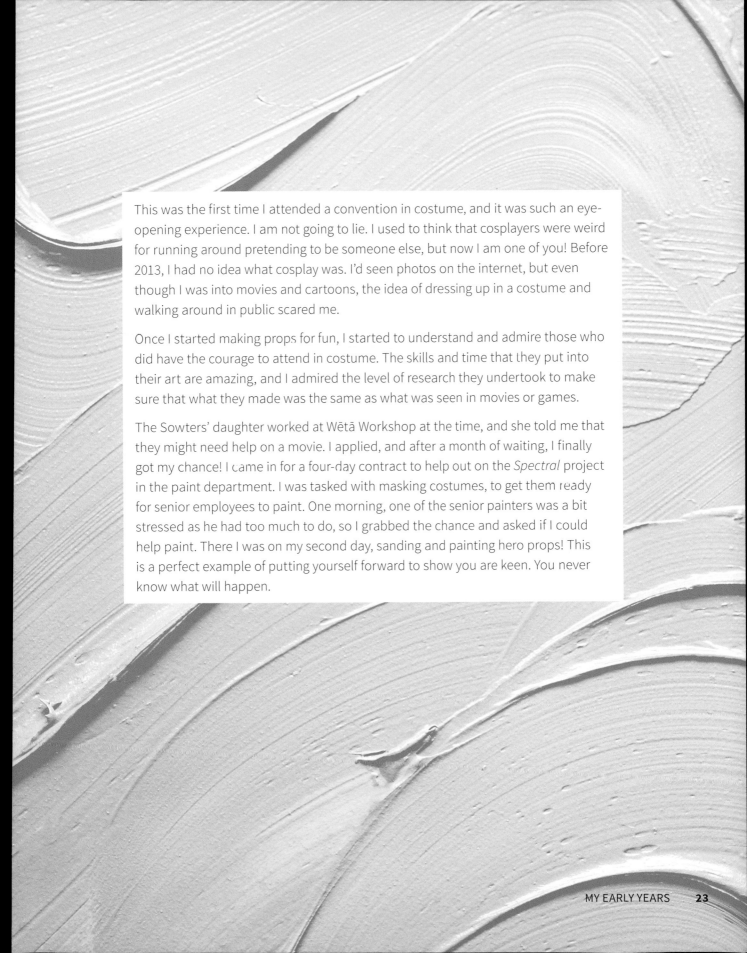

This was the first time I attended a convention in costume, and it was such an eye-opening experience. I am not going to lie. I used to think that cosplayers were weird for running around pretending to be someone else, but now I am one of you! Before 2013, I had no idea what cosplay was. I'd seen photos on the internet, but even though I was into movies and cartoons, the idea of dressing up in a costume and walking around in public scared me.

Once I started making props for fun, I started to understand and admire those who did have the courage to attend in costume. The skills and time that they put into their art are amazing, and I admired the level of research they undertook to make sure that what they made was the same as what was seen in movies or games.

The Sowters' daughter worked at Wētā Workshop at the time, and she told me that they might need help on a movie. I applied, and after a month of waiting, I finally got my chance! I came in for a four-day contract to help out on the *Spectral* project in the paint department. I was tasked with masking costumes, to get them ready for senior employees to paint. One morning, one of the senior painters was a bit stressed as he had too much to do, so I grabbed the chance and asked if I could help paint. There I was on my second day, sanding and painting hero props! This is a perfect example of putting yourself forward to show you are keen. You never know what will happen.

FINDING INSPIRATION

IN TV, CARTOONS, AND MOVIES

COSPLAYER: Spicythaidesign

COSTUME: Nova from Marvel

Photo by Sylvie Kirkman

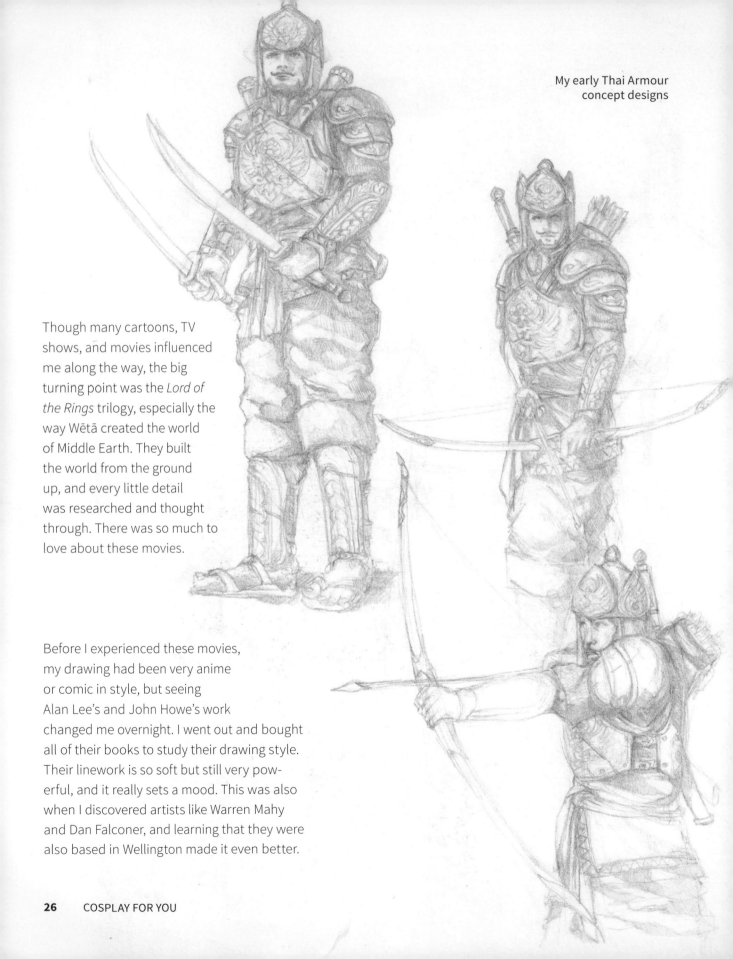

My early Thai Armour
concept designs

Though many cartoons, TV shows, and movies influenced me along the way, the big turning point was the *Lord of the Rings* trilogy, especially the way Wētā created the world of Middle Earth. They built the world from the ground up, and every little detail was researched and thought through. There was so much to love about these movies.

Before I experienced these movies, my drawing had been very anime or comic in style, but seeing Alan Lee's and John Howe's work changed me overnight. I went out and bought all of their books to study their drawing style. Their linework is so soft but still very powerful, and it really sets a mood. This was also when I discovered artists like Warren Mahy and Dan Falconer, and learning that they were also based in Wellington made it even better.

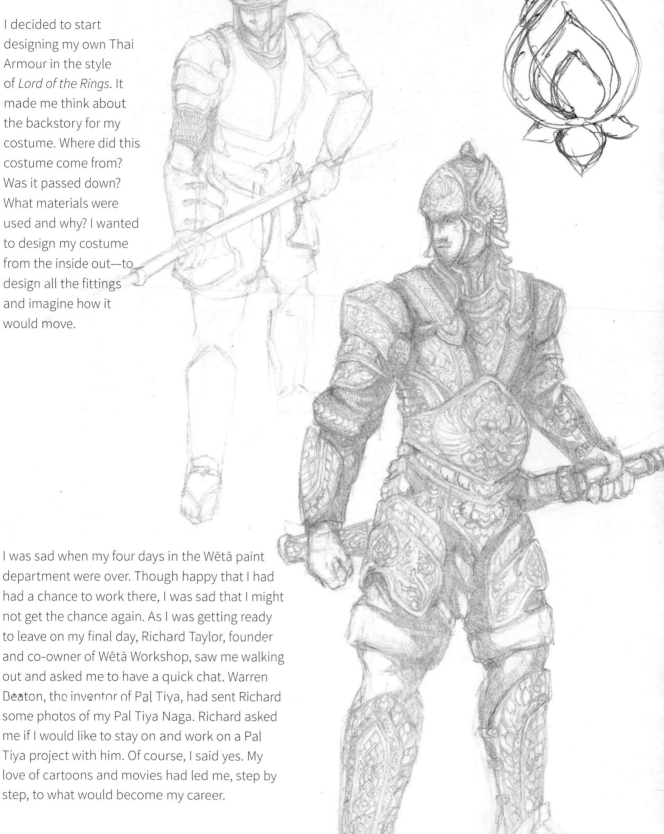

I decided to start designing my own Thai Armour in the style of *Lord of the Rings*. It made me think about the backstory for my costume. Where did this costume come from? Was it passed down? What materials were used and why? I wanted to design my costume from the inside out—to design all the fittings and imagine how it would move.

I was sad when my four days in the Wētā paint department were over. Though happy that I had had a chance to work there, I was sad that I might not get the chance again. As I was getting ready to leave on my final day, Richard Taylor, founder and co-owner of Wētā Workshop, saw me walking out and asked me to have a quick chat. Warren Beaton, the inventor of Paļ Tiya, had sent Richard some photos of my Pal Tiya Naga. Richard asked me if I would like to stay on and work on a Pal Tiya project with him. Of course, I said yes. My love of cartoons and movies had led me, step by step, to what would become my career.

MY MAKER HEROES

Warren Beaton entertains fans and educates them on sculpting with tinfoil.

There are a few people I would like to acknowledge, because without them I would not be doing what I am doing today. Some of them are people I look up to in the maker community who laid down the path for me to follow. These makers offered me so much guidance over the years and directly helped shape me into the maker I am today.

I am super lucky to have Warren and Kim Beaton as mentors. They are both extremely passionate about making. They have been working in the film industry for a long time, and Warren has worked on many iconic TV shows and movies like *The Matrix*, *Mighty Morphin Power Rangers: The Movie*, *Ultraman*, and *The Lord of the Rings*, to name just a few. Kim worked on *The Hobbit*. They are always direct. If they feel an idea isn't great, they aren't afraid to say so. I really enjoy hanging with them and hearing stories of Warren's past jobs and making cool Pal Tiya sculptures with Kim. Without their ongoing encouragement and pushing me to be the best maker I can be, I wouldn't have landed a job at Wētā Workshop.

Kim and me with my latest Pal Tiya tabletop sculpture, based on Thai Naga and Garuda

Sir Richard Taylor, Creative Director at Wētā Workshop

Photo by Wētā Workshop

As I got to know Richard Taylor and his wife, Tina, I was amazed by how friendly and approachable they are. They hold a high place in the New Zealand film industry, but I find them to be the most down-to-earth people. One story comes to mind. One day, as I was packing up and getting ready to leave for the day, Richard popped in with two backpackers. He said he'd been driving home and saw them waiting in the rain for the bus and offered them a ride into town. When they realised who was offering, they shared that they were big fans of Wētā Workshop. Richard then turned the car around and gave them a personal tour. How cool is this guy? I want to take this opportunity to say thank you to Richard for giving me the chance to stay at Wētā and for the support he always gives for what I do at work and outside work.

My workmates at Wētā have been some of my greatest sources of inspiration. For the past seven years, I have learned so much. Each day that I go to work I learn something new. To give just one example, Bryce Curtis was invaluable in teaching me to use closed-cell polyethylene foam, known in the workshop as black foam. Early on in my time at Wētā, I was working on a personal costume of Erebor Dwarf armour. I'd been trying to make the helmet out of EVA foam, but Bryce suggested black foam as a better medium. I was hooked. Without that early tip from Bryce, I wouldn't be doing what I do now.

Bryce, a.k.a. the black foam master, helping me get ready for a work event. I'm wearing my Erebor Dwarf costume, inspired by *The Hobbit*

ONLINE INFLUENCES

A number of talented makers and artists can be found online, sharing their work and their expertise. Andrew Cook, known online as Andrew DFT, is a New Zealand maker, and he was the first cosplay maker I followed. Andrew would craft most of his guns from closed-cell extruded polystyrene foam using a small craft knife, sand them, and then finish them with acrylic paint. As I was living in a one-bedroom apartment at the time, his methods were perfect for me.

Andrew DFT with his Covenant Carbine from *Halo*

Photo by Andrew Cook

I found Bill Doran of Punished Props around the same time. His videos often feature him working with MDF, medium-density fibreboard, which is his specialty. His videos are very easy to follow, and he often offers free blueprints so you can follow along. In the early years, his wife, Britt, was behind the camera, but I've now gotten to know both of them and I enjoy her builds just as much as Bill's MDF builds. In 2017 I was staying with Eric Jones of Coregeek Creations, and we decided to visit Bill and Britt, who would be busy putting last-minute touch-ups on their props for BlizzCon. We turned up at 11 p.m. with pizza, and Eric and I jumped in to help them finish up their props. It was a night to remember.

Punished Props

Photo by Punished Props

Eric Jones is the sanding master. Eric is known for his love of sanding, and all his props and costumes are super smooth with a beautiful finish. Where most of us might be happy with "yeah, it's good enough," Eric is a perfectionist. We'd been talking on Facebook for about a year or two before we met at PAX West in 2015. He pretty much saved my life. You will read later about how I, in my Dwarf costume, was unable to fit into the hotel shuttle. In short, I had to walk to the convention on a very hot day. I wasn't doing very well by the time I arrived, and Eric got me water and looked after me! What a legend.

The master of sanding,
Eric Jones of Coregeek Creations
Photo by Photo Geek Girl

The one and only Evilted giving me
some of his cosplay photos

Another online connection is Ted Smith, aka Evilted. I first came across Ted's videos when I was beginning to make my Thai *Halo* Spartan helmet. Ted has a super-simple and easy-to-follow tinfoil and duct tape patterning video, and to this day when someone asks me how to make a helmet, I recommend that video. Ted is also a bit of a hero to me because he used to work in the film industry. He was super kind to host me for a few days in 2017, and I loved hearing all about his past film projects and the people he worked with.

Cosplay can be a lonely hobby, so it pays to connect with someone who shares your passion. Svetlana and Benni from Kamui Cosplay are a dream team. They complement each other so well—Svetlana with her larger-than-life personality and Benni with his awesome sense of humour. I started following Kamui Cosplay when I first tried out Wonderflex, a thermoplastic that you can shape by adding heat. I was amazed by all the cool stuff she made just by using a heat gun. Because I was living in a small apartment, this was perfect! To be able to stay with them for a couple of days and see how they work was a big eye-opener. I learned how hard it is to make cosplay your full-time job. Everything they do supports their business, and it shows as next-level focus.

Photo by Benjamin Schwarz and Svetlana Quindt from Kamui Cosplay

COSPLAYER:
Downen Creative
Studios

COSTUME: Hela
from Marvel
Cinematic Universe

*Photo by Downen
Photography*

Another cosplay couple is Beverly Downen of Downen Creative Studios and her husband, Brett Downen of Downen Photography. Beverly has made so many amazing costumes and is one of the founding members of a group called SheProp!, a forum where female, nonbinary, and transgender cosplayers can be comfortable and find a unique and supportive community within the cosplay world. Beverly shares a lot of online tutorials on how she creates her costumes. Having amazing costumes is great, but you need to have equally amazing photos, and Brett has this base covered. Brett is not only an awesome photographer; he is also a cool guy to be around. I got to spend a lot of time with them after Emerald City Comic Con 2019. And we had a blast!

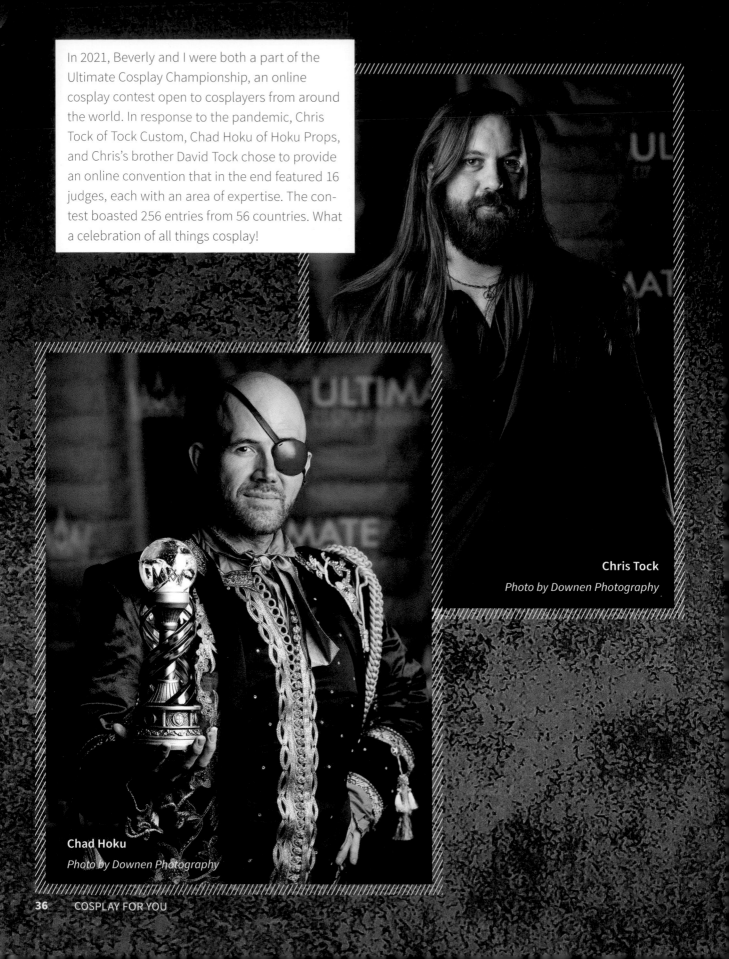

In 2021, Beverly and I were both a part of the Ultimate Cosplay Championship, an online cosplay contest open to cosplayers from around the world. In response to the pandemic, Chris Tock of Tock Custom, Chad Hoku of Hoku Props, and Chris's brother David Tock chose to provide an online convention that in the end featured 16 judges, each with an area of expertise. The contest boasted 256 entries from 56 countries. What a celebration of all things cosplay!

Chris Tock
Photo by Downen Photography

Chad Hoku
Photo by Downen Photography

THE COSPLAY COMMUNITY

I'm frequently asked if I will ever make cosplay my full-time job. While I never say never, for now I'm happy to keep it as a hobby as much as I can. I take my cosplay very seriously, but I enjoy putting out content when I want to, not because I have to. However, the biggest reason is that I love what I do at Wētā Workshop. I get to work with world-class makers and, more importantly, learn from them. I then love sharing my new knowledge with the cosplay community. To me, knowledge is something that needs to be shared, and the more we can share our love of making with the world, the stronger we'll be able to keep the maker community.

Talking about world-class makers, I have to mention the King of Cosplay, Adam Savage. Adam champions and promotes cosplay, and because of his work, cosplay isn't just an underground activity; it is mainstream. I believe that he is the reason that cosplay is so popular and cool—well, cooler. Many people know him from his work on *MythBusters* and *Tested*, but to watch him walk a convention floor and see the enjoyment on his face when he is in costume is inspiring, and because of that people want to be a part of the cosplay community.

Adam is one of the biggest supporters of the maker community, and a number of cosplayers and makers have been featured on *Tested*. Recently, Adam has been organising a lot of online workshops as part of SiliCon. Each workshop includes video instructions, all the required

materials, and the opportunity to ask questions of the instructor. I was asked to teach a workshop on making foam vambraces without glue. I just want to take this opportunity to say thank you, Adam, for all you have done.

Along the way, so many people have taught me, inspired me, and shaped me into the maker I am. Thanks to these and many other makers, I now have an arsenal of skills and knowledge that I enjoy passing on to new makers and other cosplayers. Cosplay is a very community-based hobby, but it can also be competitive. No one learns on their own; it takes a community, learning from others, fostering relationships, and growing together. Don't be afraid to ask for help or to reach out to people with higher-level skills.

REIMA

One thing that I am well known for is putting my own twist on existing costume designs. That spin can be anything from adding Thai design elements to completely reimagining a design. What I enjoy the most about costuming is problem-solving—to be able to be the first to make something that has not been made before.

A costume redesign is also often prompted by the need to be able to move freely and attend cons comfortably. Many characters start with inhuman proportions or oversized armour, and I redesign costumes to marry function with form. There is nothing worse than a costume that doesn't allow you to walk or take restroom breaks!

GINE

WHITE FLAME

OVER LAP
TO STOP
UNDER SHIRT
FROM LIFTING
UP TO THIGH

This concept sketch of what will eventually become my Red Mandalorian costume from *Star Wars* is a great illustration of my design process.

MY PROCESS OF REDESIGNING

I like to choose costumes that no one else has done—for example, my version of Nova from Marvel. Even though people have made Nova costumes based on the comic or cartoon, I haven't seen anyone reimagine Nova as if he were a part of the Marvel Cinematic Universe (MCU). I reviewed the current MCU costume designs and imagined how I could make Nova look like he fits into this universe. I took inspiration from Nova Corps from *Guardians of the Galaxy* and the *Captain Marvel* elite Kree military uniform. I've always wanted to make Nova. I really enjoy his character in the *Ultimate Spider-Man* animated series, and I wanted to capture that feel for my costume. To achieve this, I kept the silhouette very slimline, with no bulky, oversized armour pieces. My first step on any costume is to sketch.

Early concept drawing of my Nova armour from Marvel

In 2015, I made my Red Mandalorian costume, which was a fun opportunity to add my take on an iconic costume. What I love about all the Mandalorian designs people have created is that each Mandalorian character has its own story. I didn't want to make another set of Boba Fett armour; I wanted to make one unique to me. The illustration at the beginning of this chapter shows my initial concept drawings for the Red Mandalorian costume (pages 38-39). I added Thai motifs to several portions of the armour, and I chose red and black, of course, for my colour palette.

I like to sketch out every costume I work on, because drawing gives me an opportunity to figure out how the costume could be made and envision each layer and the internal attachments.

COSPLAYER: Spicythaidesign

COSTUME: Red Mandalorian from the Star Wars franchise

As this was a costume from Star Wars, I knew that there could be backlash from purists, but I created this costume for myself and I was going to do it my way.

REDESIGNING FOR WEARABILITY

I had so much fun making my Thai Red Spartan. I dove into the world of *Halo*—feet first. I've always loved the look and the stories of the Orbital Drop Shock Troopers (ODST), the *Halo* universe's special forces. They often get dropped behind enemy lines and fight their way out. I really enjoy the look of their armour; it's simple with beautiful technical details, but it's designed for an in-game setting. In the real world, their armour couldn't move the way it should. On a person, the chest armour is so wide the wearer couldn't cross their arms, and the vambraces so high they couldn't bend their arms. I redesigned my costume to make this armour super wearable while still giving me the finished look I wanted. In Creating Body Armour (page 90), I'll explain how I accommodate both an oversized look and comfort.

COSPLAYER: Spicythaidesign

COSTUME: Orbital Drop Shock Troopers from *Halo*

My redesigned costume allows for free movement

Photo by Richard Heaps

In 2019, I captained the New Zealand team in the Overwatch Cosplay Battle in Pax, Australia. I chose Victoria Gridley (The Gridler) and Johanna Otto (Chimaera) as my teammates. In this competition, teams choose two characters, and the public votes on which character the team will make. We were given Reaper, in his Lu Bu skin, as our project. As this was a contest costume, we needed to keep the aesthetic of the character. While our main goal was to maintain the silhouette of the character, the inhuman proportions would need to be adjusted to make the costume both ergonomic and wearable. We first had to adjust the neck. Reaper has a very long neck, and we did think about having his head attached on top of my head, with an opaque panel so I could look out of his neck. We decided that would make the headpiece very heavy and wouldn't allow for movement. We opted to shorten the neck of the character in exchange for more comfort and realistic movement.

Because we needed to keep as close to the original character as possible, it was important that the rest of the costume reflect the complex look of the Reaper. One thing that I truly enjoy is looking at a design and trying to figure out how that costume could be constructed. I start by imagining each layer of the costume. The more layers you add, the more detail you can show. For Reaper, I started with the undersuit and designed each layer of the costume out to the top, most decorative, layer. Along the way, it was important to decide which materials would offer the right textures and look, and where and how to put in rigging to attach the armour pieces. In this costume we used both hook-and-loop tape and D-rings. We used hook-and-loop tape for most of the connections but substituted D-rings where we needed strong connections, like the connection from the pauldrons to the shoulders.

The illustration below demonstrates my approach to layering. The areas in red became the soft fabric or leather underlayer of the costume. The blue portions are soft EVA foam that begin to give the costume shape while remaining softer and allowing potentially problematic areas of the costume, such as the spikes, to be worn safely. The yellow shows the portions we created out of rigid EVA foam, which provides the structure and the sharper lines we needed. The final layer, in green, added the finest details and was made using Worbla.

ORIGINAL DESIGNS

I'm not having a dig at people who want to make a screen-accurate *Iron Man* or *Deadpool* costume. There is nothing wrong with striving to make an exact replica of a costume as it exists in canon. It is a cool feeling to own a replica of a costume or a character that you love. I respect people who go out of their way to source the exact material, find just the right texture, or craft the right boots. Over the years I have gotten to know the Star Wars 501st Legion, New Zealand Outpost 42. Their dedication to exacting detail and their work for charity are admirable.

COSPLAYER:
From left to right, KiwiCaptainRex, Spicythaidesign, and Sam Parkin, CX 77255

COSTUMES: Storm Troopers from Star Wars

At the 501st Outpost 42 booth, Armageddon Expo in Wellington, New Zealand

As artists we are encouraged to express ourselves, to show off our uniqueness and individuality. I feel the same way about cosplay. At work, my job is to create the costumes assigned to me, but cosplay is still a hobby for me. It is something that I enjoy, so I don't want to stress out about getting the right materials or exact measurements. I like the freedom to do what I want.

COSPLAYER:
Spicythaidesign

COSTUME: Warlock
from *Destiny*

The second version
of my Warlock costume

Photo by Madeleine Buddo

My series of *Destiny* costumes, consisting of three Warlocks and one Titan, is a great example of how I approach costume design. I've made the Warlock three times. My first Warlock, made in 2014, was based on the Hanuman figure from Thai mythology. The Hanuman figure is always depicted in white, which set my colour palette. I also pulled the three spikes from the Hanuman helmet into my interpretation of the Warlock, just like the Hanuman Khon mask in the Ramakien drama.

Hanuman Ramakien costume
worn by a performer

Photo by K-Smile love

I normally like to sketch out my costumes, but I was having trouble figuring out what the helmet would look like, so I decided to grab some oil-based clay and sculpt the helmet in 3D, hoping that it would help me visualise the helmet. If your first approach isn't working, try another.

When I remade the costume in 2015, I tried to put myself in the mind of the character and make my design choices based on what the character would want. The black and gold looked cool, and the darker shades would have been better camouflage.

I was having trouble conceptualising what the helmet would look like in 2D, so I decided to do a 3D sculpt.

COSPLAYER: Spicythaidesign
COSTUME: Warlock from *Destiny*
I made all of the armour pieces using EVA foam because it is a light and easy-to-get material.

Photo by Christopher Menges

My third Warlock costume and my Titan costume were where I truly freed my creativity. The game *Destiny* really encourages you to customise your character, so why not do the same in cosplay? While searching online for costume ideas for the 2017 BlizzCon convention, I came across an image of a Demon Hunter from *Diablo 3*. Partway through designing the costume, I realised that the Demon Hunter costume would look amazing on my Warlock! As the parent companies behind *Destiny* and *Diablo* had recently merged, it seemed perfect to create a mash-up of the two! I not only wanted to create a costume mash-up of these two characters, I wanted to add my own twist—a bit of my Thai culture. By taking inspiration from all the armour in the game, adapting what was necessary to fit a human frame, and adding Thai-inspired details, I was able to develop a costume that I feel really kept with the spirit of the game while enriching my experience.

COSPLAYER: Spicythaidesign

COSTUME: Mashup of Warlock from *Destiny* and Demon Hunter from *Diablo 3*

The helmet and breastplate were carried over from my second Warlock costume; all the rest is new.

Photo by Madeleine Buddo

COSPLAYER: Spicythaidesign

COSTUME: Mashup of Warlock from *Destiny* and Demon Hunter from *Diablo 3*

To achieve the authentic look of engraved armour, I used a heat gun and a metal sculpting tool to deboss my designs into the outer layer of Worbla armour.

Photo by Madeleine Buddo

Before I made my Titan, all of my costumes had been characters that were slimmer, sleeker, and more agile. My challenge in creating the Titan in 2015 was to achieve the bulky look required while still creating a wearable and detail-laden costume. It took all of the tricks I'd acquired from my previous costumes, and all of the amazing techniques I'd learned at Wētā and from other makers, to create a Titan that was bulky and menacing while still allowing sufficient range of motion.

As I've already shared, the main reason I favour creating original designs is that it allows me to celebrate my Thai heritage. It makes the costume truly my own, and I become more attached to the finished costume. It allows me to imagine the backstory of each costume. Every mark has a story, and if I make a mistake, nobody knows!

COSTUME: Titan from *Destiny*
Digital concept drawing of my *Destiny* "Thai-tin"

COSPLAYER: Spicythaidesign
COSTUME: Titan from *Destiny*
The iconic pose of the Ramakien character Hanuman that the armour is based on
Photo by Amp Sripimanwat

I feel my Thai Armour is my best work yet. Heavily inspired by both the *Lord of the Rings* trilogy and *King Naresuan*, I wanted to be sure to pay homage to both movies by getting the design historically correct. It was important to me that it not only looked like authentic antique armour but that the costume allowed for good movement.

To make sure my look was authentic, I sourced all of the fabrics directly from Thailand. I felt it was very important to do this because locally available fabrics couldn't replicate the look I envisioned. The fabrics I imported featured beautiful details and, of course, an authentic look.

I decided to make the armour out of Worbla rather than foam. Being quite light, foam is a great material, but to get the strength I needed, the foam would have to have been too thick to create the sleeker look and feel I wanted. Many would choose to sandwich a layer of foam in between two layers of Worbla. Instead, I opted to omit the foam and combine a layer of Worbla Finest Art, which is brown, with a layer of Worbla Black Art. I made a mould, sometimes referred to as a former, out of closed-cell polyethylene foam and used it to heat form the two layers of Worbla into the correct shapes for my armour pieces. The armour turned out very strong.

For me, the icing on the cake was the detail I achieved on the leather belts. I remember when I first saw all of the *Lord of the Rings* armour in person. A lot of costumes look great from afar, but with the *Lord of the Rings* costumes, when you get close, the myriad tiny details are revealed.

COSPLAYER: Spicythaidesign
COSTUME: Thai Armour

This is a close-up view of several armour plates.

Photo by Madeleine Buddo

The last reason for creating a unique design is that it allows you to stand out in the crowd. That can be both a good and a bad thing. With a completely unique costume, you might end up explaining who you are and your backstory repeatedly. On the positive side, you look great and no one will ever have the same costume as you; people will stop and ask who you are. An original costume is a true conversation starter. To me, this is one of the best things about cosplay and the reason why I started cosplaying in the first place. It allows me the opportunity to start conversations about making and exchange techniques and ideas with other makers, and to meet like-minded people and get feedback from them. I've made many lifelong friendships and even found business opportunities through conversations begun because of an original design.

TOOLS AND MATERIALS

I often get asked about my favourite tools, which materials I prefer to work with, and how I choose materials for various costume components. I hope this chapter will answer those questions. As I explain in this chapter, when I am working on a costume that should have a handmade look, I favour working by hand—for example, drawing and cutting templates by hand so the finished product has a handcrafted look. When I want my costume to look machine-made, I select power tools and machining to get the intended aesthetic.

COSPLAYER: Spicythaidesign
COSTUME: Thai Armour

Photo by Christina Phillips Photography

A WORD ON SAFETY

When using paints, chemicals, or adhesives, always be sure to read and follow all of the manufacturer's safety instructions.

It is important to protect yourself whenever you are cutting, sanding, or working with materials that can off-gas. Small pieces of material could detach and injure your eye, or you could inhale fumes or dust. To protect myself I favour a full respirator mask, as it does double duty as eye and lung protection. If you choose not to wear a full mask, be sure to use safety glasses when cutting and sanding and a respirator mask when around dust or fumes. When using power tools, it is always best to wear safety earmuffs.

INDISPENSABLE TOOLS

There are several tools that I find myself reaching for frequently that are perfect for working with a number of different materials. These are my go-to tools.

CUTTING AND SHAPING TOOLS

I don't necessarily purchase the most expensive tools, but I am careful to choose tools that have some key features that allow me to use them to their best advantage, and I select tools that are well made so they will last longer.

A heat gun is the most important tool you will use as a maker. A heat gun with variable temperature control is a must-have for working with Worbla and EVA foam.

Strong, sharp heavy-duty scissors are essential for many tasks. I also frequently use a box cutter for larger cuts, and I favour a solid metal scalpel for cutting in smaller spaces or for detail work.

Detail belt sander

A detail belt sander is key to working with Worbla, foam, and sometimes leather. I use a ⅜" × 21" (9mm × 533mm) belt sander when I want a sharp edge or a smooth finish. I reach for an orbital sander when I have a large area that needs to be smoothed. When working with leather, I find sanders useful if I need to rough up the surface of the leather for glueing or for adding battle damage.

A rotary tool allows me to get sharp edges or achieve a smooth finish on a costume or prop when working on smaller or harder-to-reach spaces. I use a flex-shaft attachment, which allows me to get into tight spaces that the detail belt sander or the hand sander can't reach. I only use two bits, the sanding band and the Dremel 952 ⅜″ (9.5mm) aluminum oxide grinding stone.

Sanding drum

Aluminum oxide grinding stone

MARKING TOOLS

I use gel ink ballpoint pens in black and silver to mark cutting lines and details. I pick up the silver when marking black materials and prefer the black when marking on lighter-coloured materials. Ballpoint pen ink and even permanent markers can bleed through paint. When you're working on a piece that is to be painted, mark on the back side when possible, or be sure to sand off the marker before painting.

WORBLA

Worbla is a brand of sheet thermoplastics manufactured by a German company called Cast4Art. Thermoplastics become mouldable or pliable when heated and harden when cooled. A hairdryer won't do the trick; you'll need a heat gun to work with this material. Worbla is available in a variety of forms, each designed for various applications. The three I use most are Worbla's Finest Art, Black Art, and Pearly Art.

Finest Art is brown and was the first Worbla product. I find it super easy to work with. It has great self-adhesion, but it is highly textured. If you want a smooth surface, you would have to do a lot of sanding.

Black Art is, as the name suggests, black in colour, and what I like the most about this product is the colour. I don't have to prime my pieces black before painting, and it is a bit smoother than Finest Art. The texture is very similar to leather. It has to be heated to a higher degree than Finest Art to get adhesion.

Pearly Art is white, and it is super smooth. It is amazing for creating highly detailed pieces. Pearly Art does not need to be heated much before becoming pliable.

From left to right, Worbla's Finest Art, Black Art, Pearly Art, the reverse side of Pearly Art

I created this sculpture using Worbla Pearly Art.

WHY I LIKE USING WORBLA

I would describe using Worbla as crafting and sculpting at the same time. Worbla adheres to itself so there is no messy glueing, and it is nontoxic so you can use it at home. It is a better choice for making thin armour than EVA foam. Two layers of Worbla are enough to create strong armour, and it is easier to get the desired look. Possibly the best thing about Worbla is that there is hardly any waste. All your off-cuts can be reheated and used again. The same cannot be said of EVA foam.

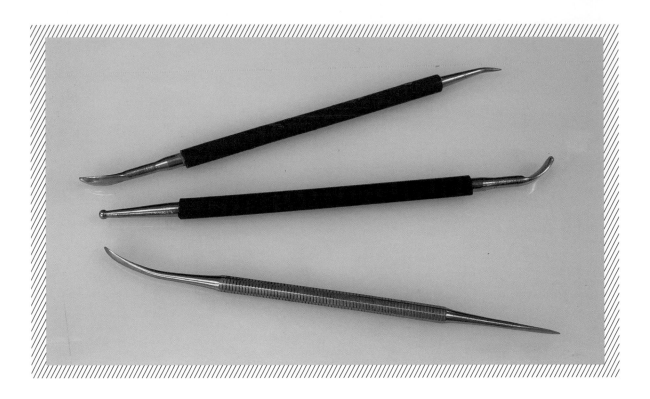

I use metal sculpting tools when working with Worbla rather than tools made of wood or plastic. Wooden tools can impart a wood grain to your finished piece, and plastic tools could melt or bend if heated. Metal tools also give a nice sharp finish.

I found Worbla hard to work with at first, but after a good six months of trial and error, it became one of my go-to materials. To this day I am always trying out new techniques for using Worbla. It is super important to take your time with Worbla. You don't want to rush it. For example, if you are creating a piece of chest armour, you don't want to heat up the whole piece. Start from the middle and slowly work your way outwards. I never heat an area bigger than my hand. Some people wear gloves while working with Worbla, worrying that they'll burn their hands. I think if you need to wear gloves, you've overheated the material. I heat it until it is hot but not uncomfortable to touch. Worbla does cool down very quickly, but it is better to heat it more frequently—working one small area at a time—than to overheat it. When I am creating details, I often let the Worbla cool down almost completely, which allows me to get very sharp edges.

WEATHER WARNING!
Note that Worbla is a temperature-sensitive material. When worn outside in very hot temperatures it can change shape over time, and it can bend and warp when left in a hot car.

ADDING DETAILS TO WORBLA

I like to keep it old school and start with pencil and paper. I use heavyweight paper rather than photocopy paper, or I back a piece of photocopy paper with a layer of masking tape to prevent the paper from tearing easily. I begin by drawing out my design. For this example, I'll be using a vambrace I created as part of my Thai Armour costume. Because the detail on my vambrace is mirrored (the same on both sides), I only have to draw one side, which cut my time in half. *fig A*

When I am satisfied with the drawn design, I use a scalpel to cut out the design, creating a template. If my design contains any very delicate details, I am careful to use a sharp blade and back those areas with tape for additional stability, and I'm careful not to make any additional cuts that would result in the loss of the finer details. *fig B*

Next, I transfer the design to the Worbla using a silver or black pen, whichever colour is appropriate for the colour of Worbla I'm using. To be sure the design is identical on both sides, I flip the template over, overlapping the centre of the design to ensure correct placement. *fig C*

A

B

C

Rather than creating the detail on my piece by adding layers of Worbla, I sculpt the detail into the original layer of Worbla. My technique is inspired by my grandma's silver drinking bowl. Her bowl had the most beautiful hammer-forged Thai design, and I want to achieve that same look for my vambrace. I want it to look like it was hand-hammered out of a single piece of metal.

To achieve a forged look, I begin by heating a small area of the vambrace, making sure to heat from the bottom and the top evenly. I then slowly push up from the bottom with my finger in the centre of the design while pushing down along the lines of the design with my sculpting tool. I work slowly, without overheating the Worbla, and repeat this step until I've added all of the lines to my design. *fig D*

To finish the piece, I cut a thin strip of Worbla that is slightly longer than the perimeter of my piece. I carefully adhere the strip around the outside edge using my heat gun. Rather than heating up the piece I just detailed, I use the heat gun to gently heat the Worbla strip and then apply the strip to my vambrace. I feel it is important to bevel and soften the edges of armour pieces to achieve a realistic look. It is a step that many cosplayers omit, and it can make a piece that took days to create look unfinished or amateur. *figs E-F*

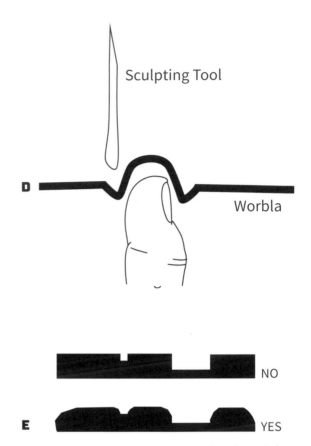

Sculpting Tool

D

Worbla

NO

E

YES

In the top example, the added strip has been left as it was applied. The bottom example shows the edges after they have been beveled, which in my opinion looks a lot more realistic.

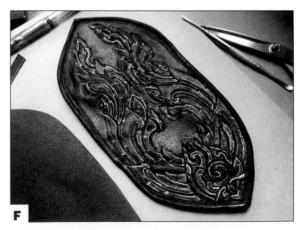

F

The final vambrace with edging applied

CREATING CRISP LINES

Many makers find it impossible to get clean, straight edges on Worbla pieces—and it can be difficult. However, there is a way to do it. Avoid the temptation to try heating and sculpting to get crisp lines. Instead, reach for a detail belt sander. What I like about this tool is that I can get consistent, sharp edges. Because the end of the belt is so narrow, I can reach most areas of my costume piece. To avoid building up residue on the belt, turn the speed down a bit on the belt sander. Where I can't reach with the belt sander, I use my rotary tool.

My Sub-Zero mask from *Mortal Kombat* is a great example of getting clean, sharp details using Worbla. I first carved the mask form out of closed-cell polyethylene foam, being careful to ensure that the lines of the foam mask were clean and sharp. Worbla can hide small blemishes but will show larger imperfections.

I heated the Worbla and carefully draped it over my foam mask form, being sure to work from the centre mouth hole outwards to prevent tearing. While it is possible to patch holes in Worbla, it's easier to get it right the first time.

In the image to the right, you can see how Worbla normally looks. The edges are very rounded and the surface is a bit rough.

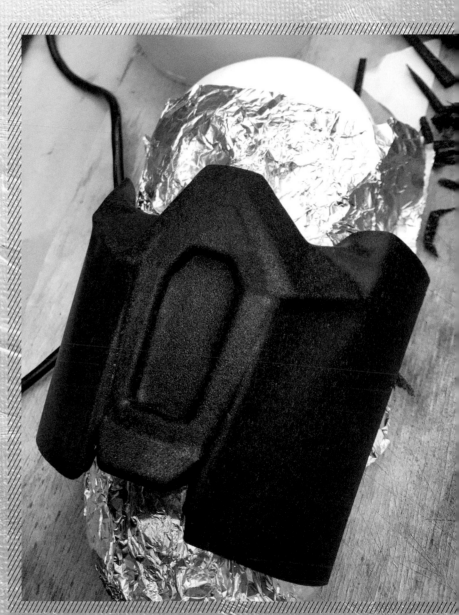

I next used my detail belt sander and rotary tool to smooth all of the surfaces and shape the lines and edges to achieve a crisp metal appearance. I allowed some of the edges to remain rounded where I wanted to simulate wear and tear.

The finished mask

ACHIEVING ORGANIC EFFECTS

While I do use Worbla to create armour pieces with a metal appearance, Worbla was made to create an organic look. If you are trying to simulate wood, bone, or other natural materials, you can't overlook Worbla. It was the obvious choice when I made my Tobi mask from *Naruto* (right). I layered the material in the same way that wood grows, being careful not to add too many layers. I didn't want the mask to be too thick. I sculpted the edges using a heat gun and a sharp metal sculpting tool, making sure not to overheat the Worbla.

I used the same technique on the horns of this demon mask. As you can see, Worbla is great for organic shapes and objects.

These helmets are all made of EVA foam.

WHEN EVA FOAM IS THE RIGHT CHOICE

When I first began making costumes, I used EVA foam floor mats. They're cheap, easy to get, and great for beginners, but the quality of the foam can vary. Floor mats can contain air bubbles and be textured on the underside—though some makers, for example, *Mass Effect* cosplayers, have incorporated the textured side as a costume feature. I now generally prefer to use high-density EVA foam, which allows me to create a lot more detail. However, I incorporate low-density foam where I want the bottom layer of a costume piece to be softer and more comfortable.

When working with foam, I have found that to get the desired look and feel I must treat the foam as I would the material I am mimicking. For example, if my goal is to make a helmet that appears to be made of metal, I try to think of the foam as metal and plan my steps accordingly, including the way I shape it and connect the pieces. To shape foam, I turn to my heat gun. I use a low heat setting. Once the piece is heated, I shape the foam over my knee or occasionally over a DIY anvil. I should note that I will also use my heat gun to heat seal the foam before painting.

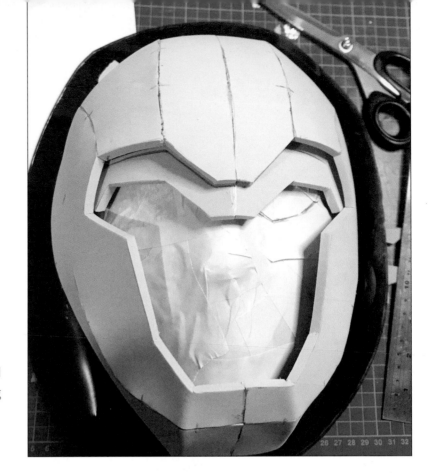

My Greek-inspired helmet is a good example of how I approach working with foam. As a blacksmith would with metal, I started by creating and shaping the base layer, keeping that base nice and simple. I slowly built up the details one layer at a time.

As when working with Worbla, I prefer to trace my design onto heavy-duty paper and use a utility knife to cut out the details to create a template. Rather than cutting out both sides of a mirrored design, I prefer to cut out just one side and any centre elements. I transfer one side of the design and then flip the template and transfer the other side to achieve a symmetrical look. Be sure to line up the centre elements!

When it is time to connect your pieces, use contact cement, the best adhesive to use with foam. Working in a well-ventilated area, mark the area that you want to glue and add a good layer of glue to both surfaces to be glued. Let the glue dry for 10–15 minutes, or use your heat gun on low or a hairdryer to speed up the drying time. This first layer seals the foam and allows for a tighter bond. Apply a second layer of cement and allow the glue to dry till just tacky; then stick the two surfaces together. As noted earlier, always read and follow all safety instructions on your chosen adhesive.

Because the design on this helmet was super intricate, I cut all the lines in at an angle using a small scalpel. Cutting at an angle resulted in beveled edges. I was able to finish most of the edges with the scalpel, but I softened the rougher cuts with my rotary tool. The smaller burrs will disappear when I use the heat gun to heat seal the helmet prior to painting.

Compare the two sides. The right side is finished, but on the left I haven't yet done the bevel cut. Notice the difference between the two finishes.

It is good to know when to stop. I could have added more detail, but I left some areas plain to give the eyes a place to rest.

WHEN LEATHER IS BEST

Leather is super strong, and I love the look of real leather. For my costumes, I like to use genuine leather for belts and vambraces. Belts simply look more authentic when made of leather, and vambraces are a costume element I find myself taking off and putting on frequently. When made with foam they tend to rip with wear and tear. I like the look I get with a leather vambrace—how it covers my whole forearm and how the leather has a natural feel. When a costume requires lacing, I also tend to use leather because other materials can quickly wear out and can't stand much strain. *fig A*

Rigging—the straps and attachments in a costume that hold the various components together and allow the wearer to get in and out of the item with minimal difficulty and without altering the appearance of the garment—is an element I almost always create using leather. For these parts of a costume, strength and durability are essential. To be honest, I enjoy working with leather and I try to use it whenever I can. *fig B*

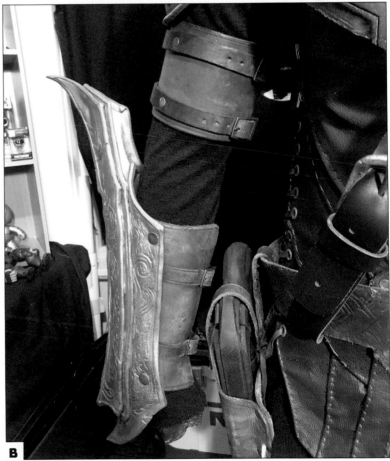

LEATHER TOOLS

There are so many leather tools available and they all do a wonderful job, but there are a handful I turn to over and over.

As when working with any of my other favoured materials, I feel that finishing the edges of leather costume pieces is an important and often overlooked step in creating a realistic look. To do so I use an edge beveler and an adjustable groover. An edge beveler is a great tool for getting softer edges on your leather pieces. Different sizes of beveling tools are available, depending on the angle you want to achieve. I like to bevel both the smooth and rough sides of my leather pieces. *figs A-B*

An adjustable groover allows you to add a consistent line detail along each beveled edge. I prefer an adjustable groover because it is handy when I want to change the depth or width of the groove. *fig C*

Using both a beveling tool and an adjustable groover along the edges of your pieces gives you a nice, soft edge with a hand-worked appearance. *fig D*

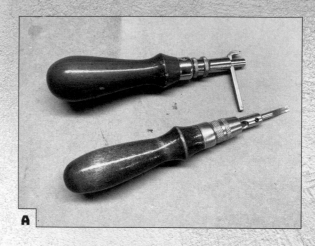

A

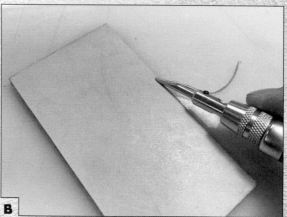

B

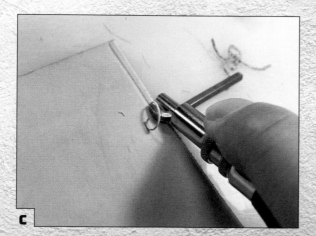

C

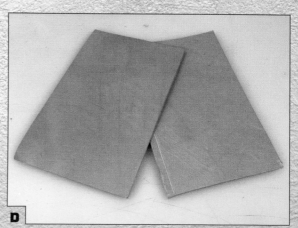

D

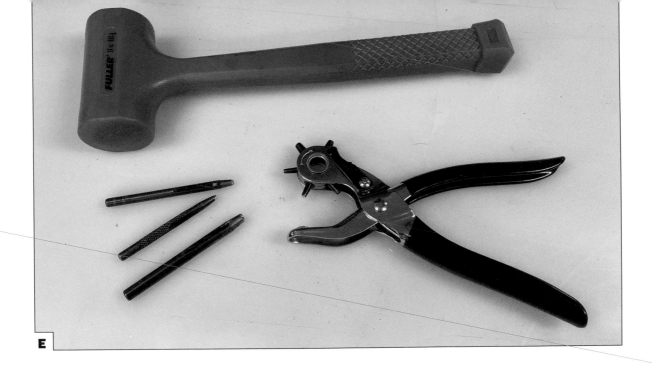

E

I also cannot do without a leather hole punch. The name says it all: it makes neat and clean holes in leather. You can get a version similar to a paper hole punch, where you place the leather between two jaws and squeeze, or you can get a punch that you place over the leather and hit with a mallet. If you choose the second type of punch, it is important to select the correct weight of mallet. Before you choose your mallet, try out a few in different weights. You will want a rubber or sand mallet, and it should be heavy enough to offer the strength you need yet light enough for you to wield comfortably. Select one that is large enough to be easy to aim; too small and you'll have to aim carefully, which could result in smashed fingers if you miss. Don't ever use a metal hammer with a hole punch. *fig E*

Contact cement formulated for use on leather is essential. Always read and follow all safety warnings on the label! Glueing leather is simple, but it is important to follow the steps carefully to get a strong join:

1. Working in a well-ventilated area, mark the area that you want to glue on both pieces.

2. Rough up any smooth surfaces on the leather before you apply glue. Contact cement needs a rough surface to adhere to or it will peel off.

3. Put a layer of glue on each glueing surface, being super careful not to go over your marked lines.

4. Let the glue dry for 10–15 minutes, or use your heat gun on low or a hairdryer to speed up the process. When heating glue, always use a respirator mask. This first layer seals or primes the leather; the second layer is where the magic happens!

5. Add a second layer of glue and allow it to dry until it is tacky, around 3–4 minutes.

6. Place the two surfaces together and push down on both sides to make sure they stick.

! GLUE CAREFULLY

When glueing leather, be very careful not to get glue on any surfaces that you are not actually glueing! If you are planning to dye your piece later, any areas with glue will not take dye.

WORKING WITH LEATHER

Adding designs and patterns to leather gives the costume an authentic look. It is always great to see a costume from afar and admire how good it looks, but there is something special when closer inspection reveals beautiful little details.

There are several ways to add designs to leather. The most time-consuming method of adding decorative detail to leather is through traditional leatherworking, using a set of leather tools to deboss and carve designs directly into the leather. While traditional leatherwork is a lot of fun, it can take months and is not always feasible. There are entire books on leatherwork, so I won't outline the process here, but if you have a lot of time on your hands, it is worth diving in!

To create the design on this belt, I sketched my design onto the leather using a pencil and then hand carved the design into the leather using an adjustable leather swivel knife.

The simplest way to add detail to leather is to stamp the leather, as I did on my Thai Armour (cover). There are a couple of methods I use for creating stamps. One method is to pour melted wax into a flat baking tray to create a wax base. I then use a ball-tip sculpting tool to carve out my design. Next, I pour casting resin onto the wax to create a stamp. Note that any item used when crafting with resin should no longer be used for food preparation. Remember to always read and follow all safety instructions for the products you use.

A second method to create a leather stamp is to commission a custom acrylic stamp. For my Thai Armour, I created a vector design using Adobe Illustrator. If you are not familiar with design software, you can commission a custom illustration.

Once the design was final, I got it laser etched onto acrylic. My design required two passes of etching to achieve the desired depth. *fig A*

Whichever method you use to create your template, debossing the design onto the leather is the same. First, thoroughly wet the piece of leather for a few seconds. Second, use a press to apply enough pressure to stamp the design into the leather. *fig B*

Once the design is stamped into the leather, you can use alcohol-based leather dye to dye the pieces to the desired shade. Because the leather is wet during the stamping process and leather is removed during carving, dyeing should be the last step. Be sure to stamp and dye extra pieces in case some of the pieces take the dye differently! *fig C*

ADDING HARDWARE

When using leather rigging, I opt for metal buckles. They are a real component rather than a fabrication, so they work every time and are simple to apply. I prefer to use centre bar buckles and heel bar buckles.

Both types of buckles are attached in the same manner, though you will need an extra step to finish the job with a heel bar buckle. First, determine the size of the strap you will need. Buckles are measured not by their exterior length or width but by the width of the prong hole. If you will be using a strap that is 1″(2.5cm) wide, then you will need a 1″ (2.5cm) buckle. When you have the right size buckle, cut your strap to the correct width and length. I tend to cut my straps slightly narrower than the buckle measurement to make it easier to work with. Once the strap is cut, I use my trusty edge beveler to clean up all of the edges. *fig A*

Next, I mark a linewhere I need the prong of the buckle to come through the strap. Using your leather hole punch, punch a hole on each end of the marked line. Use a utility knife to remove the leather between the two holes. *fig B*

Put the prong through the strap. *fig C*

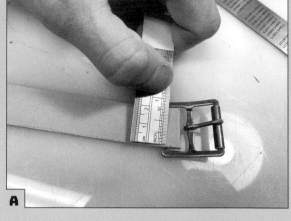

A

B

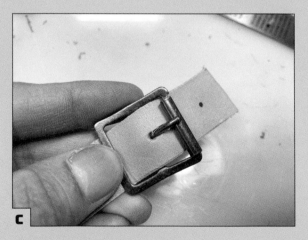

C

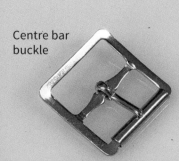

Centre bar buckle

Heel bar buckle

D

I'm lucky to have access to a kick press, but you can easily add a rivet by hand with a rivet setter.

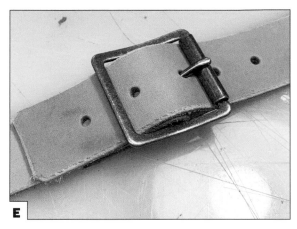

E

Note how the centre bar buckle secures the strap end.

Fold the end of the leather piece around the bar of the buckle and secure the two ends of the strip with a rivet. *fig D*

If you are using a heel bar buckle, you will need one additional step. While a centre bar buckle has a full frame to hold down the end of the strap, a heel bar buckle does not, so you will need to add a strap loop to contain the strap end. *figs E-F*

You can add the loop either inside or outside the fold that holds the centre bar. *figs G-H*

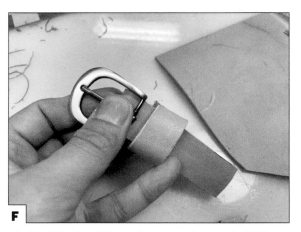

F

The heel bar buckle needs a strap loop to hold the strap end.

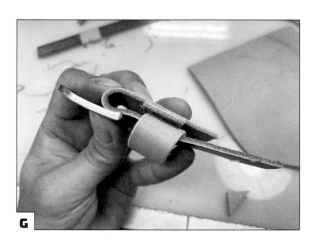

G

The strap loop inside the fold

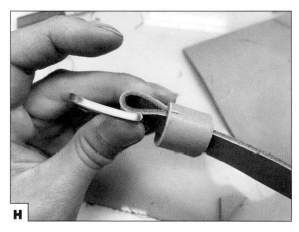

H

The strap loop outside the fold

The choice depends on how much room you have and your desired finished look. I tend to capture the loops inside my straps. I find it a lot cleaner, and it keeps the loops from catching on things. *figs I-J*

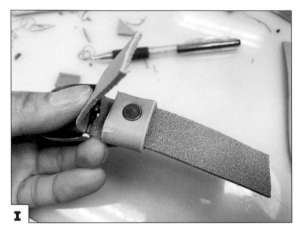

I

Capturing the loop inside the buckle fold is a more secure connection.

J

Leaving the loop free of the buckle fold allows for much more adjustment for capturing the end of a longer belt.

Lastly, I use my leather hole punch to punch holes in either the other end of the strap when I am creating a belt out of a looped strap, or in a separate piece of leather when I am adding the straps to two separate pieces. *figs K-L*

K

Using my leather punch tool to punch holes in the other end of my belt

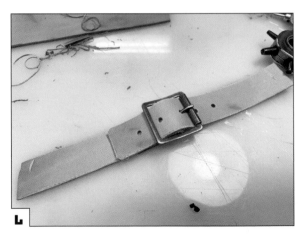

L

Straps ready to add to two separate pieces

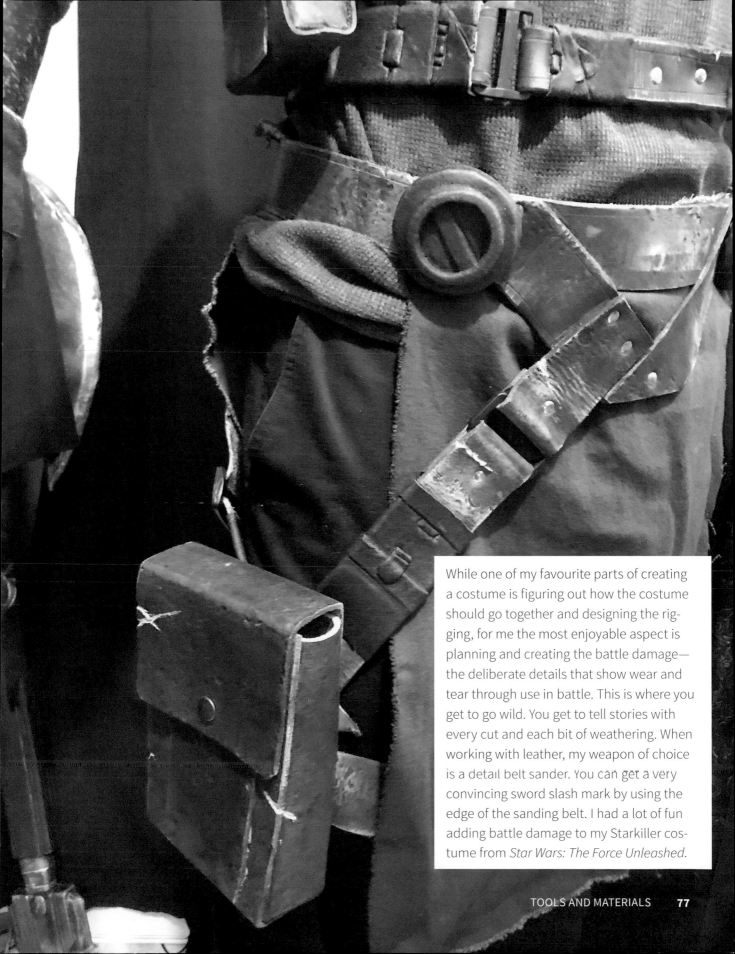

While one of my favourite parts of creating a costume is figuring out how the costume should go together and designing the rigging, for me the most enjoyable aspect is planning and creating the battle damage—the deliberate details that show wear and tear through use in battle. This is where you get to go wild. You get to tell stories with every cut and each bit of weathering. When working with leather, my weapon of choice is a detail belt sander. You can get a very convincing sword slash mark by using the edge of the sanding belt. I had a lot of fun adding battle damage to my Starkiller costume from *Star Wars: The Force Unleashed*.

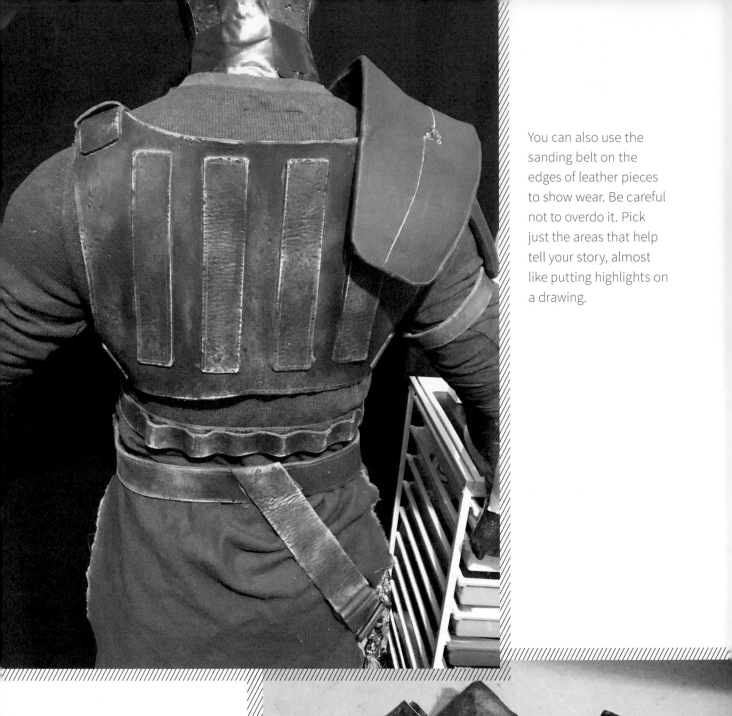

You can also use the sanding belt on the edges of leather pieces to show wear. Be careful not to overdo it. Pick just the areas that help tell your story, almost like putting highlights on a drawing.

The last, and most fun, technique that I use is to simply wet the leather by spritzing it with water, lay the piece smooth side down on a rough bit of concrete, and hit the leather with a mallet.

Cosplay as a Community

You don't have to be an expert in everything. When faced with an aspect of a costume for which you don't have the required expertise, or the necessary tools are out of reach, it is okay to ask for help!

Cosplay is not just a hobby; it is a community with a wealth of people with all types of skills, expertise, and equipment. For example, I'm not the best at using 3D printing software. While I'm known for and passionate about my handmade costumes and props, there are times when using a 3D printer is a better choice. For example, when making my version of a Nova costume from Marvel, I knew I wanted the helmet to be perfectly smooth and symmetrical. Working by hand I could get close, but to really get the effect I wanted I needed to 3D print this helmet.

COSPLAYER: Spicythaidesign

COSTUME: Nova from Marvel Cinematic Universe

My take on Nova. I needed the help of my cosplay community to create the helmet I envisioned.

Photo by Sylvie Kirkman

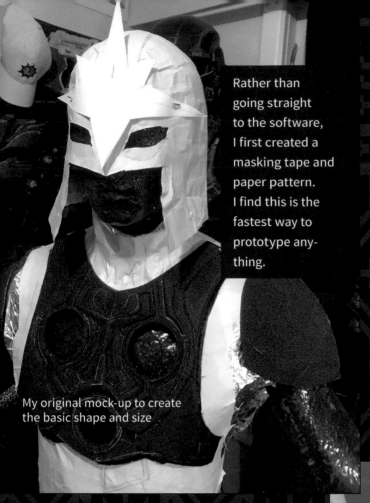

Rather than going straight to the software, I first created a masking tape and paper pattern. I find this is the fastest way to prototype anything.

My original mock-up to create the basic shape and size

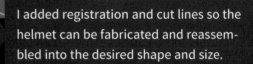

I added registration and cut lines so the helmet can be fabricated and reassembled into the desired shape and size.

Next, I sculpted the helmet out of closed-cell polyethylene foam (known in the industry as black foam), which is easy to carve with a sharp knife, to ensure that the helmet would be the right size. This is a technique we often use at Wētā Workshop.

At this point, I knew I needed an assist! I recruited my workmate Ryan to translate my prototype helmet into a 3D file that could be used to 3D print the helmet.

The helmet was printed in segments. Once it was printed, I took out all the supports and glued the helmet together using quick-cure adhesive.

After many hours of filing and sanding, the print lines were gone and the helmet was assembled and super smooth, ready for paint and battle damage.

My helmet was finally done, complete with paint and battle damage. I truly believe that the cosplay community is filled with talented people and that by working together we can create some amazing projects.

MAKER'S GUIDE

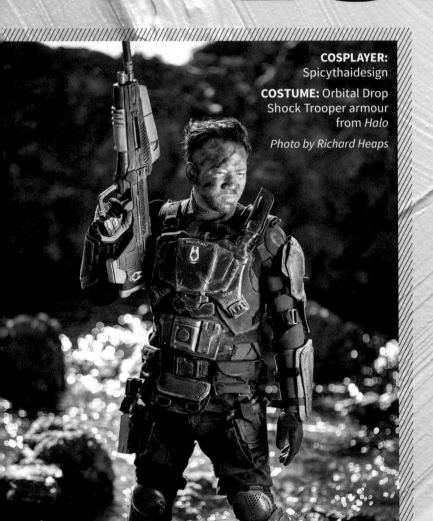

COSPLAYER: Spicythaidesign

COSTUME: Orbital Drop Shock Trooper armour from *Halo*

Photo by Richard Heaps

As makers, we all tend to jump in and start by creating the hero piece, usually the helmet or breastplate, even though the more sensible plan would be to begin with the least-seen elements. Be prepared to remake this central piece if you find that by the time you've finished the rest of the costume, your skills have really improved!

FROM HEAD TO TOE

I have a tried-and-true approach to creating the main aspects of my costumes. In this chapter, I'll walk you through how I prefer to make my helmets, breastplates, pauldrons, ab plates, backplates, vambraces, greaves, and thigh armour.

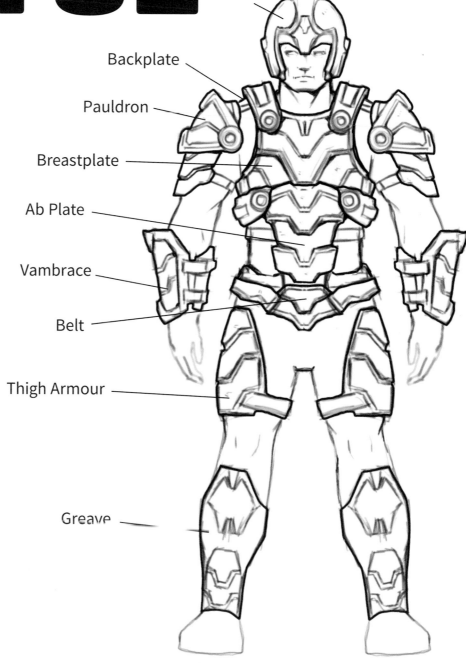

Helmet

Backplate

Pauldron

Breastplate

Ab Plate

Vambrace

Belt

Thigh Armour

Greave

CRAFTING HELMETS

I believe that a helmet can be the hardest part of a costume to make. But I've found a method of creating helmets that works for me every time! While they can be simple or complex, they all start with a simple shape. When tackling a complex helmet, once you can break it down into simple, easy-to-manage shapes, you are sorted.

My first step, made famous by makers such as Evilted and Punished Props, is to use what I call the tinfoil and masking tape technique to capture the basic shape of the helmet. To do this, I wrap my head in tinfoil and then apply a layer of masking tape over the top. This is a sure way to know that the helmet will fit. I prefer my helmets to be very tight. I want my helmets to look sleek and stream-lined, not ending up too bulky and looking like a bobblehead! No pain, no gain, right?

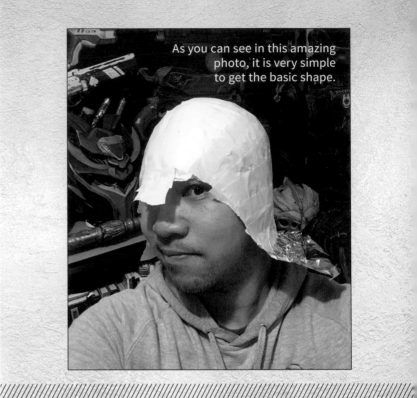

As you can see in this amazing photo, it is very simple to get the basic shape.

CREATING THE HELMET BASE

My next step will be to create a template. The main idea is to determine how to split the main shape apart into workable pieces that can be individually shaped and then fitted back together to achieve the intended look, feel, and shape while fitting comfortably on my head.

First, I draw in the lines where I will need to cut the individual pieces and add registration marks. Registration marks will help you later correctly align your pieces for assembly. You should add two or more registration lines along each seam. Before I cut out the template pieces, I label them *left* and *right*, *front* and *back*, so that I don't end up glueing the wrong pieces together and having to start over. *fig A*

I then carefully cut out the template along the lines. I now have a template that fits my head perfectly, but I'm not done. I must take into account the thickness of the material I'm using. For example, if I select 4mm EVA foam, I have to add 4mm (³⁄₁₆″) to my template pieces on each edge that will be attached to another piece. This allows me to account for the surface area necessary when glueing the pieces together. If I'm using a thin material, such as a couple of layers of Worbla, this is not as critical, but it is still best to increase the size of your templates a little bit to be sure your final helmet is not too tight. It is better to make the helmet pieces a bit large and find that you have to trim them a bit than it is to end up with a helmet that is too tight! Adding additional pieces to increase the size of a helmet is time-intensive and often does not result in the look you want.

Now I transfer my rough tinfoil and masking tape template pieces onto some card stock. I use the

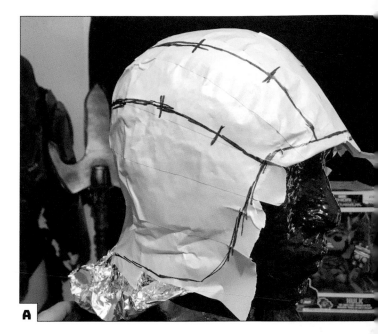

A

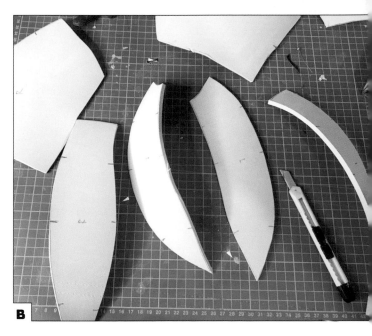

B

card stock templates to cut out all of the helmet pieces from EVA foam, being careful to transfer the registration marks and my labels for front and back and left and right to assist with later assembly. *fig B*

Many makers prefer to heat form their foam pieces to the desired shape before glueing. While I do preshape my pieces if the helmet involves very complex curves, for the most part I skip this step. If you opt to heat form your pieces before glueing, remember to use proper ventilation and safety equipment.

I'm now ready to glue it all together. For a refresher on glueing, see When EVA Foam Is the Right Choice (page 66). The first key to successfully glueing your pieces together is to ensure that the edges of all the pieces are smooth and clean. Because I prefer my helmets to fit snugly, I need strong seams. It is best to glue all the pieces for one half together at the same time, followed by the other (independently creating both halves), and then glue the two halves together. *fig C*

The key to a perfect seam is to begin with a clean edge, avoid using too much glue, and make sure to apply the glue evenly across the full surface to be glued. I carefully align my registration marks, and then I push the two halves together to create a clean join between the two halves of the helmet. *figs D-E*

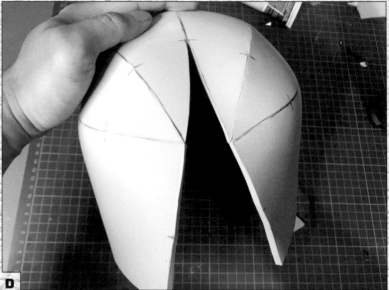

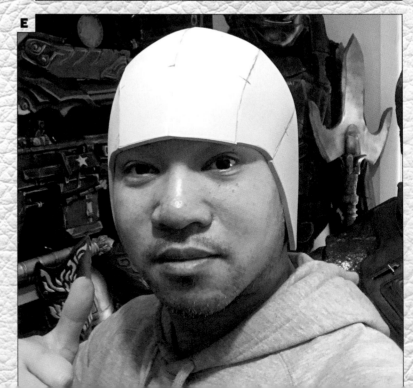

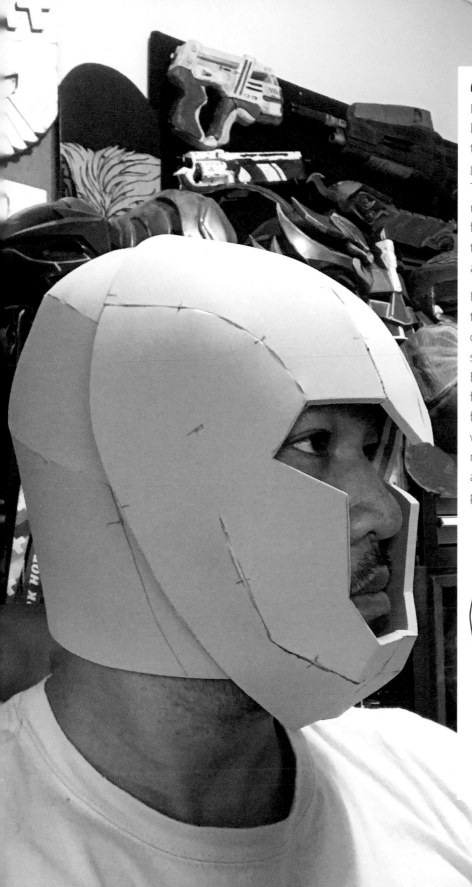

ADDING LAYERS

Next, I must determine what additional layers are needed to create my masterpiece. For this helmet, I decided to go for a very simple open face mask. To create the front face mask portion, I repeat the previous steps using a head form rather than my own head. Once the face mask is done, I am ready to adhere it to the base.

I layer the foam face mask pieces onto the base, making sure that I have plenty of overlap between the two pieces to securely glue the two halves together. Because the helmet is made of EVA foam, I can take it on and off with the front piece glued to the base. If you are working with a more rigid material, you may need to add hook-and-loop tape or another attachment method that is less permanent than glue.

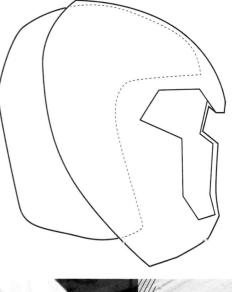

Next, I add another layer of face mask, this time made of Worbla. To match the shape of the foam layer, I heat form the Worbla using a face form. In this case, I used a vacuum-forming mask mould to achieve the correct shape.

Finally, I add additional details to the Worbla and foam layers, working layer by layer to create more detail, and attach the inner Worbla face mask to the outer foam face mask using contact cement.

My Reaper helmet, inspired by Reaper from *Overwatch*, is another good example of how I use my construction methods, but this time to create something with a more fantastical shape. After studying several pieces of concept art and in-game screenshots, I started by sculpting the helmet out of tinfoil. Tinfoil is a great sculpting material because it is super malleable. All you need is a hot glue gun to glue the portions of tinfoil to each other, working carefully to avoid burns. As usual when I sculpt a piece out of tinfoil, I began by creating a base that mirrors the shape of my face. Next, I added a layer of masking tape to help maintain this shape as I worked. I then added layers of tinfoil to achieve the look and shape of my finished mask. The second layer of tinfoil can easily be removed for patterning.

Next, I wrapped the whole tinfoil helmet with masking tape, being sure to apply the tape as smoothly as possible. Then I drew in the cut lines using a marker. I made sure to put in registration marks so I could later remember which pieces were attached to which other pieces. I now had all of my pattern pieces. *figs A-B*

Using the pattern pieces I'd just created, I transferred the patterns onto EVA foam, cut out the foam pieces, and glued them together piece by piece, paying close attention to be sure that all the registration marks were lined up, as the helmet is quite complex. *fig C*

As you can see from the beginning phases of this Reaper helmet, you can use these techniques to create any helmet you can imagine. Just remember that the most important thing is to always use and line up registration marks and label all pattern pieces, or you can easily go astray!

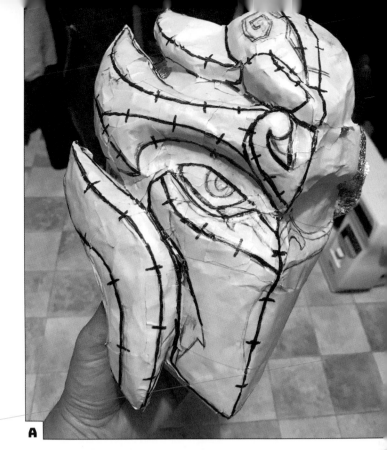

A

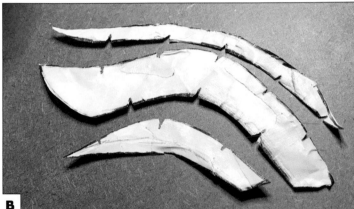

B

C

CREATING BODY ARMOUR

The key to making comfortable and movable armour starts with a well-scaled breastplate and pauldrons. I learned this the hard way in 2014 when I made my Dwarf costume from *The Hobbit*. It looked great and was almost identical to the costumes in the movie, but I could hardly move!

It was hard to walk while wearing the costume, and because the breastplate was so big, I couldn't sit down. If I dropped my axe, I had no way to pick it up. Aside from issues of comfort and mobility, I do still love this costume. I wore it on my first U.S. trip to PAX West and Dragon Con. It was a very hot day, around 90°F (32°C). I suited up in my costume and went down to the lobby to await the shuttle. When the van turned up, I realised that I was too wide for the van and there was no way I could sit down. I had to walk. After walking for half an hour in that heat, I was exhausted. After that trip, I told myself I would never be so uncomfortable again.

In addition to the other issues, it was a nightmare to pack the big Dwarf armour in a suitcase. Since then, I've designed my costumes so they can be easily disassembled and nested for packing and travel. This and the use of a hard-sided suitcase help me avoid damage in transit.

Let's start creating our armour with the most important piece, the breastplate. I know it would be more logical to start with the easiest part, for example, the vambraces, but you and I know we always start with the helmet and the breastplate, even if it means we may have to remake them at the end because our skills improved so much as we made the full costume.

COSPLAYER: Spicythaidesign
COSTUME: Erebor Dwarf from *The Hobbit*
Photo by Richard Heaps

COSTUMES: From left to right, Thai Armour and Orbital Drop Shock Trooper from *Halo*

THE BREASTPLATE

I came up with a few rules that I always follow to ensure that my armour allows mobility. First, I always begin with the breastplate. It's important not to make it too wide. Be sure you can fold your arms across your chest and touch the opposite sides of the piece. If your breastplate is too wide, then moving your arm across your body will dislodge the breastplate. This is a big issue if your costume includes weaponry, especially guns. With an oversized breastplate, you can't hold a gun properly.

You can see an example of my approach to scale in my Red Ranger costume from *Power Rangers*. The breastplate fits me, allows for freedom of movement, and matches the look I want in my finished costume.

The illustration to the right shows a basic breastplate silhouette. *fig A*

When my costume requires a bulkier breastplate, I turn to layering as a way to add size and bulk while retaining mobility. I add a second layer under the original breastplate to increase the width and use elastic to attach the added pieces, so that when I move, the layers naturally move back and forth with my movements. This creates the illusion that the breastplate is wider than it actually is while still allowing for a normal range of motion and comfort.

If you take this approach, be sure to allow for enough overlap of the pieces so that the lower layer doesn't pop out as you move. *fig B*

For attaching the two pieces, I find that elastic is best. I often choose ¾″ (20mm) elastic and add multiple attachment points. This allows the pieces to move smoothly and to shift back to their original position naturally. To create the attachment, I make a hole in the added section and then thread the elastic through the hole and attach it to the undersides of both the added piece and the main breastplate. *fig C*

Be sure to use enough elastic tabs so your pieces move smoothly and don't slip apart. *fig D*

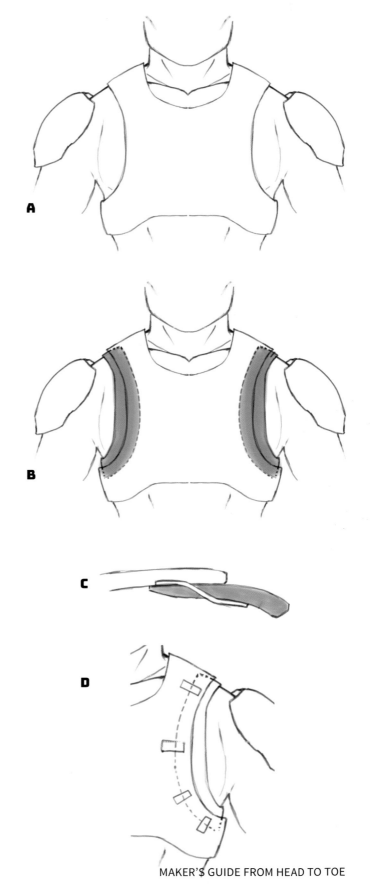

THE PAULDRONS

When it comes to designing pauldrons, there are two things to puzzle out: the overall size of the pauldrons and how you'll rig them to the breastplate. We've all seen costumes where the pauldrons are so oversized the cosplayer can't even lift their arms.

I always try to keep the pauldrons from extending into the armpit area, because pauldrons can also restrict back-and-forth arm movement if they are too wide.

When I need a longer pauldron, I again turn to layering to add additional segments called rerebraces. I create my pauldrons in several pieces and layer them to create added bulk while still allowing for movement.

In the illustration to the right, you can see the basic components of my pauldron and how I prefer to attach my pauldrons to the breastplate. As with the multipiece breastplate, I make each of the pieces large enough to allow for enough overlap so there is plenty of space to attach the straps and rigging. *fig A*

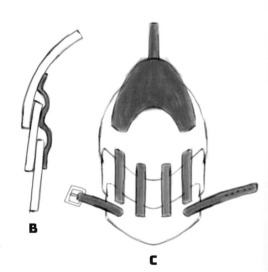

A

Most of the time I choose leather to attach the pieces of my pauldrons. Its strength means that I can use contact cement or rivets to attach the pieces for a strong bond. Also, if my costume includes other leather components, it creates a more cohesive look to also use leather to attach these pieces.

To attach the pauldrons to the costume, and to attach each piece of the pauldron to the other, I use leather strips. Notice that I don't attach the whole strip, just the ends, leaving the area between the two pieces unglued to allow the pauldron and the rerebrace to move freely over each other. *fig B*

In the last illustration, you can see the underside of a typical pauldron, complete with leather attachments. As the last step, I add my rigging with buckles at the bottom of the rerebrace, to attach the bottom of the piece to my arm. To make sure your finished costume sports buckles that face the same direction, mirror the buckle placement on each side and label which is left and right (on the underside, of course). *fig C*

B

C

THE AB PLATE

I attach the ab plate under the breastplate using a wide leather strip, in the same manner as I did with the individual sections of the pauldron. As I do with the rerebrace, I leave enough overlap so that the breastplate and the ab plate slide over each other without leaving a gap. At the bottom of the ab piece, I add another piece of leather to act as an anchor for my body armour.

I then add hook-and-loop tape to the leather anchor to allow me to attach the ab plate to my belt. There is nothing worse than walking through a con and having to pop your ab plate back in before every photo. Yes, I am speaking from experience! *fig D*

Top right is a peek at the underside of my typical assembly. You can see the placement and number of the attachment strips and the leather anchor piece. *fig E*

I made my ODST (Orbital Drop Shock Trooper armour from *Halo* using the methods described earlier.

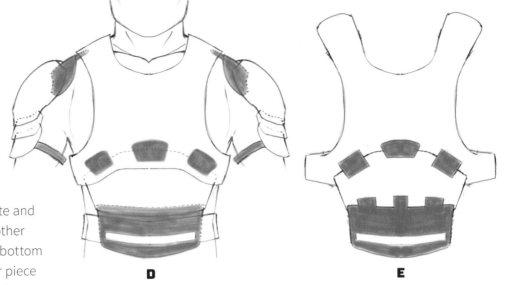

D   **E**

! **HOOK-AND-LOOP WISDOM**
Whenever you use hook-and-loop tape, make sure the hook side faces away from your body. The loop side is softer and won't scratch you if the hook-and-loop tape isn't attached exactly squarely.

COSPLAYER: Spicythaidesign

COSTUME: Orbital Drop Shock Trooper armour from *Halo*

Photo by Peter Iti of Kohika Creative

THE BACKPLATE

I create the backplate in much the same way that I do the breastplate, but it is important to note that the neckline on the backplate is higher than the neckline on the breastplate. I also make the leather anchor at the bottom much longer than the one on the ab plate; however, I do not add hook-and-loop tape. If you need to bend over to pick anything up, the longer piece accommodates the movement, but if it were secured with hook-and-loop tape it would pull up the back of your costume when you bend over. That would be very uncomfortable! *fig A*

When it comes to adding the final rigging, you can see my usual setup in the illustration below. Most of the time I get ready for a con on my own, so I need a rigging system that allows me to put on and take off my costume by myself. To make this possible, I put the shoulder buckles on the front. I also feel this adds a bit of detail to the front. I could glue the front and back together at the shoulder, making the costume even easier to put on, but it wouldn't have as authentic a look, and not glueing them together allows me to separate the front and back pieces and stack them for easy packing and storage. I make the shoulder portion of the backplate longer than the front, so it overlaps the breastplate where I have the buckles affixed. *fig B*

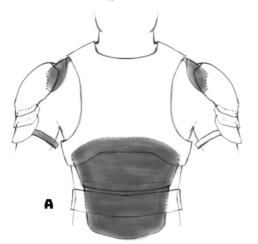

A

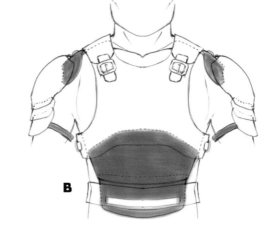

B

My approach to shaping the sides of the backplate is similar, but I allow the breastplate to overlap the backplate rather than the backplate overlapping the breastplate as I do at the shoulders. For the sides, I place the buckles on the backplate so the excess strap faces the back, keeping the look tidy. *figs C-D*

The breastplate and backplate of my Thai Armour costume were created using the principles described above.

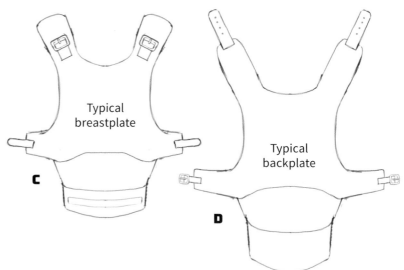

Typical breastplate

C

Typical backplate

D

COSPLAYER: Spicythaidesign
COSTUME: Thai Armour
Photo by Christina Phillips Photography

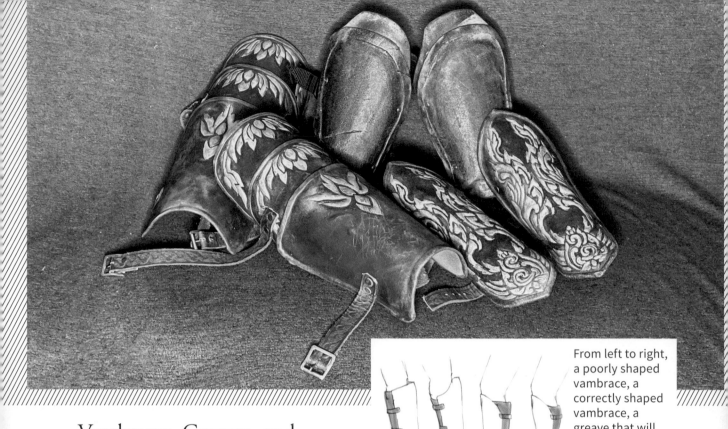

From left to right, a poorly shaped vambrace, a correctly shaped vambrace, a greave that will cause discomfort, a correctly shaped greave.

Vambraces, Greaves, and Thigh Armour

The vambraces, greaves, and thigh armour pieces are often some of the easier parts of the armour to make, but if you get them wrong they can make your experience in your costume very uncomfortable. Before you begin, you should know that the vambraces and the greaves are not tubes. If I want nice-fitting, sexy armour, I make sure that these pieces follow the curves of my forearms and calves. I begin with a heavy paper rectangle, and I cut a scoop-shaped dip out of the inner side of each vambrace, just below the elbow, to allow me to bend my arms, and the pieces are narrower at the wrist end to give a form-fitting look. Once I have the desired shape, I transfer this template to my chosen material. I favour leather for my vambraces and greaves, as these pieces can take a lot of wear and tear, but they can also be made from EVA foam. I follow the same steps to create pattern pieces for my greaves, this time sloping the piece behind and below the knee, to allow me to bend my legs, and narrowing the piece towards the ankle. I then transfer the greave patterns to my chosen material and cut them out.

Note that if you choose to add detail or decoration to these pieces, you should add that detail after the pieces are cut out but before you add the rigging. Prior to adding the detail, mark where the attachment points will be so that these do not interfere with the detail you add.

I next add a layer of leather as an underlayer on my vambraces and greaves. Leather can be very form-fitting and comfortable, and it is very strong, which makes it the best choice for rigging, as vambraces and greaves can take a lot of wear and tear. To create a fitted underlayer, I again turn to the tinfoil and masking tape technique to mould a pattern of my calves and the undersides of my forearms. I use the resulting pattern to create a template for the leather underlayer that will now look and feel like a custom piece.

Measure Twice!

It is always best to create pattern pieces of both your left and your right arms and calves, and to label these templates *left* and *right*. Due to an injury in my early 20s, my right calf is a bit smaller than my left. I once used just my right calf to create a template for this layer and could not get the left greave to fit! One arm or leg will always be dominant, so it is better to make two templates than to end up with costume pieces that don't fit.

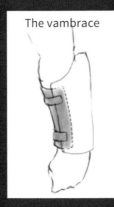

The vambrace

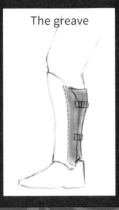

The greave

COSPLAYER:
Spicythaidesign

COSTUME: Reaper in Lu Bu skin from *Overwatch*

Photo by Josh Groom

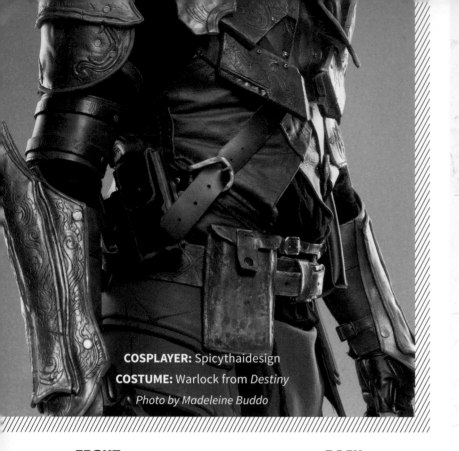

COSPLAYER: Spicythaidesign
COSTUME: Warlock from *Destiny*
Photo by Madeleine Buddo

FRONT

BACK

Lastly, I add the rigging. Though I favour leather, you can use any fastener you want. No matter what I choose, I am always careful to place the buckles or other fasteners on the outside of the leg for greaves so they do not catch and rub as I walk. And I make sure the buckles on my vambraces face the underside of my forearm so the excess strap doesn't flap around and look messy.

My Reaper costume is a good example of creating fitted vambraces.

This photo of my third Warlock costume shows the underlayer and buckle attachments for the vambraces.

When creating the thigh piece, I begin with a rectangle of thick brown paper and taper the front and back top edges to allow for free movement. I then adjust the length of the pattern piece to match the length of my thigh and make any other adjustments necessary to create the desired shape. This is now my template for making the thigh piece from either EVA foam or leather.

The thigh piece is connected to my belt at the top. On the bottom of the thigh piece, I add a couple of pieces of rigging to attach the piece to my thigh. I tend to use elastic for this portion of the rigging because it generally allows for a greater range of motion and is more comfortable. You do not want all of that rigging rubbing together as you walk around all day.

The illustrations at left show the typical configuration of my thigh pieces.

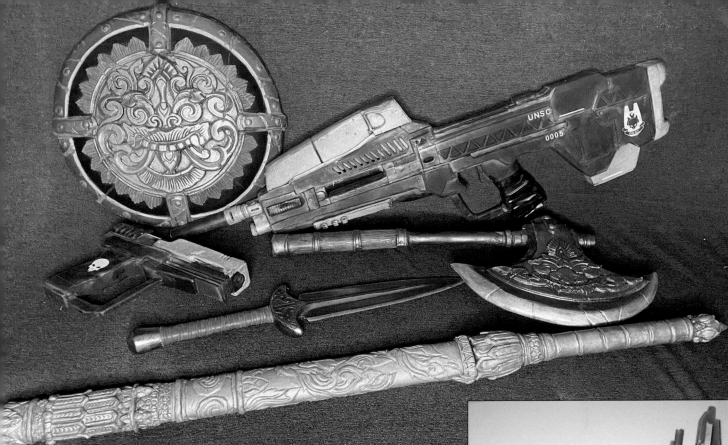

PROP MAKING

When I first began my maker career in 2013, I started by making props for fun. All my first props were made out of closed-cell extruded polystyrene foam because that is what Andrew DFT was using in his YouTube videos. I found closed-cell extruded polystyrene foam to be a beginner-friendly material. It's easy to carve with a small sharp-bladed craft knife. Here are some of the first props I made out of Styrofoam.

Spartan-scale Binary Rifle from *Halo 4*

M16 rifle with grenade launcher

My first decision in making a prop is always what base material to use. I take the finished size and weight into account when deciding on the base. In the case of the two handguns I made for my Reaper from *Overwatch* costume, I used three layers of EVA foam. I wanted to make the guns as light as possible because I'd be carrying them around all day.

I begin by making a paper template of the base layer or layers, carefully cutting them out, and then assembling the layers, making sure to mirror the layers on each side so that I end up with a 3D prop. I think that due to my background in print-making and vector illustration, I like to make my props in layers. I break down the prop I want to make and begin with the base layer, adding layer after layer until I get to the final details. *fig A*

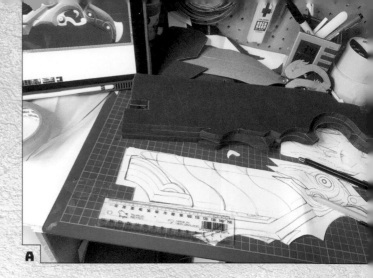

A

When I need to add curved or shaped details to my props, I rely on my trusty masking tape and tinfoil method, rather than paper, to draft the templates. *fig B*

For these two prop guns, I chose to add a layer of Worbla over the foam base for the top portion of the guns. I chose Worbla because it is closer to the finished texture I wanted and it allows for a higher level of detail. I cut a rectangle of Worbla, heat formed it over the body of the EVA foam gun, and then trimmed the excess. I did not add Worbla to the portions of the gun I'd be handling throughout the day because foam is a bit more comfortable to hold.

I started with the EVA foam base because even though I wanted the detail that Worbla offers, a prop gun made entirely of Worbla would be too heavy to carry around all day.

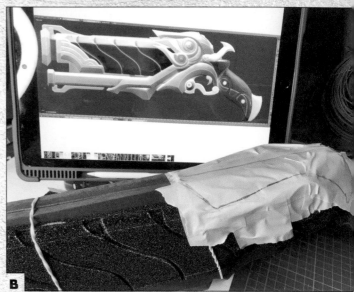

B

Reinforcing Worbla

When I add just a single layer of Worbla I sometimes worry that the Worbla will be a bit fragile. To reinforce the bond between the foam and the Worbla, I add a thin layer of urethane resin to the foam piece before heat forming the Worbla over the foam. Be sure to read and follow all manufacturer safety instructions.

Once the final details were added, I used my detail belt sander to smooth all the surfaces and sharpen the lines and edges. *fig C*

I decided to add a few more details at this point. I added a layer of Worbla Pearly Art to the grips, and I added some additional detail to the hammer using Worbla Black Art. The props were almost ready! *fig D*

After I'd painted my prop guns, my work team-mate Johanna added all the LED lights.

COSPLAYER: Spicythaidesign

COSTUME: Reaper in Lu Bu skin from *Overwatch*

Photo by Josh Groom

LET'S MAKE A SHIELD!

For the past few years, I have been privileged to be a guest tutor at Toi Whakaari: New Zealand Drama School in Wellington, where I teach students in the costume and set and props classes about working with Worbla and EVA foam building. I'm a hands-on instructor, and I usually start with having the class members make shields together. This is a great exercise, because as prop makers they could be called upon to make a shield with little notice and less budget. It is also a great illustration of my approach to prop design and creation.

What I enjoy most about teaching is that I get to see how much the students can learn in a short amount of time, and the excitement on their faces as they get the "I got it" look. Even though some of them struggle with the material at first, seeing them beginning to understand and starting to push the material is an amazing and rewarding feeling.

My EVA foam props and mask sample, made for a set and props class at Toi Whakaari

Photo by Colin Edson

To make a basic shield, I start with a piece of EVA foam gym mat. Because I use a gym mat, the size of the shield is more or less predetermined. For the shape, I want a round shield with a subtly concave shape. After cutting a perfect circle, I divide the surface into quadrants with lines from top to bottom and side to side. This makes it easier to add the design symmetrically later and helps in evenly spacing the darts. I then add small darts to remove small portions of foam evenly around the outer edge. I keep these darts small because I want a subtle curve. To get a deeper curve you would add more or deeper darts. I use contact cement to close the darts and achieve my desired shape. *fig A*

Next, I have to come up with a vision for my finished shield. For this shield, I turn again to my Thai heritage for inspiration. Online I find a photo of a cool Thai stone sculpture of a warrior holding a shield. The shield in that sculpture becomes my inspiration, and I begin by drawing the design on a piece of kraft paper. *fig B*

A

B

Now I get to start cutting! First, I cut out the largest shape in my motif. I cut out only one-half of my design because my shield is symmetrical. I trace the two quadrants of the motif onto the shield using a silver pen and then flip the templates over to transfer the motif to the other side of the shield. *fig C*

C

When I first started sculpting, I was told to sculpt with shadows—to envision what shadows will be left behind. This is a good way to envision depth and texture. As you can see in this series of photos, I use my original drawing to create separate templates, one for each layer of my design. I start with my original paper template and keep cutting it up into smaller details to achieve true depth on the surface of the shield. I try to think about how the light will hit the design and create shadows to show the depth of the design. *fig D*

D

Using a sharp knife, I cut out each layer of detail. After cutting each layer, I bevel the edges of the foam and glue the layer onto the shield using contact cement. After repeating this step a few times, I have a lot of detail on my shield! *fig E*

E

I use a sharp utility knife to sculpt in additional details and to bevel and further soften the edges and curves. I want the finished shield to resemble hand-worked metal. *fig F*

F

Close up, you can see the finer details and the soft curves.

I then add any additional fine details that I want. For this shield, I cut out small circles using a leather hole punch. *fig G*

Next, I adhere the circles to the shield where I want rivets. *fig H*

Beveling the edges is important. The end result truly resembles rivets and not just circles. I also use my rotary tool with the sanding band to add a lined effect to the outer layer of detail on the central motif. *fig I*

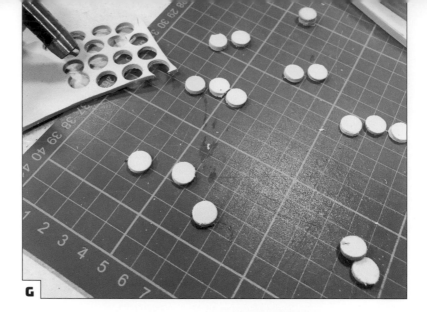

It's now time to add the battle damage. I like to imagine how each mark would have gotten on the shield and use that as my guide. This is where you can go beyond being a maker to being a storyteller! I think of how the prop would have been used, what its function was, and what might have happened to cause the damage. To add the actual damage, I use my detail belt sander and my rotary tool with the sanding band to add slash marks and gouges. I'm careful to match the lines up as I move from layer to layer of detail, and I make sure not to overdo it.

As you can see, the slash marks look as if they had come from an actual sword, slashing across layers of detail in a straight line. You can almost imagine how each bit of this damage happened!

After I've finished adding the battle damage, I use adhesive caulk to fill in any gaps and to blend the details onto the shield to make it look like one cohesive piece. *fig J*

Now it's time to seal the foam with a layer of aerosol multipurpose rubber coating. I prefer to apply a rubberized coating rather than a decoupage sealer because the it is more hard-wearing. I like to play with my finished pieces, and I have found that decoupage sealer can sometimes peel off on impact or when rubbed. When applying any aerosol, be sure to wear a respirator mask and work in a well-ventilated area. Next, I add masking tape to any portions of the shield I want to remain unpainted.

I paint the shield with gold spray paint.

I let the paint dry and then remove the tape. Peeling off the masking tape is like opening a present at Christmas!

The finishing touch is to apply an age wash. To make my age wash, I mix black and burnt sienna paints. These can be either water-based or oil paints. You can dilute the paint if desired for more subtle aging. I apply the age wash over the whole shield, allow it to dry for a bit, and then wipe off the excess paint, leaving the age wash in the details and crevices to mimic age. The longer you allow the age wash to dry, the older and more tarnished your shield will look.

Lastly, using a gold paint slightly lighter than my spray paint, I repaint portions of the top layer of detail to add some highlighted areas.

FUN TIMES AT CONS

COSPLAYERS: From left to right: Spicythaidesign, Rawbomb, and Evilted

COSTUMES: From left to right: original design base of *Destiny 2* Warlock, Warlock from *World of Warcraft*, and Red Demon original design by Evilted

My first trip to BlizzCon in Anaheim

If someone had told me back in 2013 that someday I'd travel the world meeting all the amazing makers I followed online, I'd have said they were lying. I'm now living that dream. When I first started accepting commissions in 2015, I found that most of my jobs were from the United States. I was making a lot of *Halo* props at the time and decided my first U.S. convention should be PAX West 2015. It was a great experience. I got to meet so many people that I had been connecting with on all the maker forums. The first group that I really connected with was the *Halo* game markers' group. I was amazed how they all worked together as a group and how much they enjoyed each other's company. Even though I was new, they welcomed me with open arms.

I was super lucky with my timing because Dragon Con, the world's biggest cosplay party, happens to be the weekend after PAX. I'd thought PAX was a big show, but Dragon Con was amazing. I was wowed by so many people in cosplay and partying throughout the lobbies of four different hotels in Atlanta.

Me, Rebecca, and Te Aroha at Auckland Armageddon

COSPLAYERS: From left to right: Spicythaidesign, Pinkstar14, and Te Aroha Pereiro

COSTUMES: From left to right: Warlock from *Destiny*, Alexstrasza from *World of Warcraft*, and Sailor Moon from *Sailor Moon*

While the biggest convention in Auckland, New Zealand, would be only a quarter the size of Dragon Con, for a small country we have some pretty good cons. My first experience at a New Zealand con was Auckland Armageddon expo in 2013, and my attendance there was thanks to Peter and Dee Sowter. I worked for them at their booth, Trinity Treasures, which sells replica movie and anime swords.

If I hadn't worked in the Sowters' booth, I'd never have gone to any cons. Working in the booth meant I got to be around numerous cosplayers and makers. Trinity Treasures gave me, as a shy person, the opportunity to get to know the cosplayers of New Zealand, not just those located in my hometown. This first show is also when I wore my first costume to a con! *Attending this first show really was the beginning of everything.*

A while after this show, I was able to find a small group of cosplayers and start to do meetups and take photos with them. The more I attended these meetups, the more I started to see how talented New Zealand cosplayers are. Here we are, at the bottom of the world. We might not always have all the material that the rest of the world has, but we still make amazing stuff.

For me, cons aren't just about doing demonstrations and cosplay contests; they're about the people. They're about talking and exchanging ideas and techniques with other makers.

Sophy Wong with her amazing original spacesuit. She really pushes the boundaries of 3D printing and is fascinating to talk with.

Chad's armour is a great example of out-of-scale dimensions. Check out the eagle pauldron. It's massive, but he made it work.

BlizzCon was a convention I'd always wanted to attend, and I finally did in 2017. Even though I'm not a big gamer, BlizzCon offers one of the best collections of out-of-this-world gaming cosplay. The level of accuracy in the costumes is top shelf. A lot of the characters depicted in costumes feature inhuman proportions, for example, game characters from *World of Warcraft* and *Overwatch*.

COSPLAYERS: From left to right: Bio Cosplay and Spicythaidesign

COSTUMES: From left to right: Necromancer from *Diablo III* and Warlock from *Destiny*

Not to be outdone, Sam poses in his costume.

FANTASY BASEL
THE SWISS COMIC CON

Flo and me talking about how cool it is to work at Wētā Workshop

Photo by Jeton Shali LightWav3r

COSPLAYERS: From left to right: Spicythaidesign and Polygon Forge

COSTUMES: From left to right: Nova from Marvel and Anubis Tyto, original costume inspired by Huizo_art of R-one Studio

A great example of the European level of perfection I was talking about is Polygon Forge in her Anubis Tyto costume.

In 2018, I was invited attend Fantasy Basel, the Swiss Comic Con. In my wildest dreams, I'd never imagined that I'd have the opportunity to fly to the other side of the world to hang out with my European maker friends. I was lucky to have Flo Foxworthy, head of the soft costume department at Wētā, join me for this adventure. Flo is one of the best boutique costumers in the world.

European makers are perfectionists. They don't start a project until they have found the right material with the right texture for the character they are wanting to make. Once they've found the perfect material, they may then spend months hand sewing on details to create the perfect costume.

It was so much fun travelling around Switzerland with The Egg Sisters after Fantasy Basel.

Some of the best parts of attending a convention come after the convention! After the fun and excitement of the convention itself, it is fun to relax and unwind and take in the local sights.

There is no point in playing down the fact that working for one of the world's top movie workshops does give me an advantage when it comes to standing in the cosplay world, but it's not something I strive for or enjoy. The Wētā Workshop name has given me many opportunities, but I'd like to believe my success is equally due to my hard work.

In 2019, I was offered the opportunity to attend Emerald City Comic Con for work. I had many friends who live on the West Coast of the United States, and they'd been telling me how amazing Emerald City Comic Con is, and I was excited to go. It was an honour to be there as a part of Wētā Workshop, but, more importantly, as a maker, showing other makers that it is possible to get a job in the film industry, that it is a dream worth working towards, and that it is achievable.

While attending Emerald City Comic Con I was also asked to be a part of the judging panel for the cosplay contest. My fellow judges were Philip Odango and Beverly Downen. This was the first time I'd judged a big contest, and they both helped me a lot. Philip is known for his sewing skills, I for my armour making, and Beverly for, well, everything. Between the three of us, we had all the bases covered.

This all goes to show that if you dive in, just keep going, and strive to add to your arsenal of skills, you never know where you'll end up or what opportunities may come your way. By attending conventions, even ones close to home, I began to expand my horizons and meet other makers. Once I entered the world of cosplay conventions and social media, I was amazed to find that crafting, which used to be a solitary activity, is really a global passion shared by people from around the world. Just jump in and start meeting people!

COSPLAYERS: From left to right: Philip Odango of Canvas Cosplay, Spicythaidesign, and Downen Creative Studios
COSTUMES: From left to right: Radagast the Brown from *The Hobbit,* Thai Armour, and Athena original design
Here we are at the showcase, all dressed up in our costumes.

A FINAL WORD

In my happy place
at Wētā Workshop

Photo by Angela Yip

Though I'm often asked about materials and techniques, the question I get asked most frequently is how to make a successful career from cosplay. My answer is always this: It takes a lot of hard work. Most people only see the tip of the iceberg. They don't often see all the many years of practising our craft, all the missed parties and leaving early to meet deadlines, all the late nights and weekends working on projects, all the missed time with family and friends. If your goal is to support yourself as a maker, the secret is to put in the time—a lot of time—but be aware that this career path is not a 9-to-5 job, and you'll be working odd hours and lots of them. It's a feast-or-famine industry, and at times it can be extremely rewarding when you see your finished work on the big screen or in an exhibition, but you'll also find yourself missing the occasional holiday or special occasion.

START ONLINE

My next piece of advice would be to use social media but use it well. Keep your posts positive and don't put people down. Always keep your page active and engage with others online. Comment on other people's posts because you have a genuine interest in their work, and don't be afraid to approach people you look up to. That also goes for cons. If you see someone whose work you admire, approach them and introduce yourself. They are just normal people, and I am sure they would be more than happy to talk to you. You never know where networking could take you.

When I first started making costumes and props, I knew that the only way I could improve was to ask for feedback. I did this by posting my work on social media. That opened me up to both compliments and criticism, but I have found that people tend to be supportive and want to see me succeed. When I do get unhelpful or mean comments, I just ignore them. Rather than engaging in a word war, I find that my friends tend to jump in and set them straight.

Most important of all, have fun! If you are having fun and enjoying what you do, your photos and comments will reflect that, and people will want to follow you.

GO IN PERSON

For the first two or three years of my cosplay journey, I always made costumes that had a full helmet. I was uncomfortable showing my face, not because I was ashamed of cosplaying but because I was very shy. It was hard enough trying to pose with my body, but having to worry about what my face was doing too was simply too much. In time, I started to get more and more comfortable with myself and started to design costumes that showed my face.

If your goal is to work in the film industry, reach out by email, or mail in your portfolio. If it is possible, attend a con that the company you seek to work for is also attending. Send the company a message ahead of time asking to have someone review your portfolio at the show. While dropping by unannounced can work, it's better to be sure that you'll be able to get your portfolio in front of the right people. At the con, wear a costume you have made or bring in some props you've created. It is always cooler to see pieces in person. Give them something that they can hold and look at more closely.

BE YOURSELF

In order to get noticed, you need to stand out in the crowd. When planning a new costume, think about making something unique. Pick a character that hasn't been made before, like my Nova from the Marvel comics. Nova is a known character, but he's not yet shown up in the MCU. In choosing that as my costume, I'm demonstrating my design skills by creating a Nova costume that fits well in the MCU while incorporating elements from the comics and cartoons.

This shows not only that you can redesign but that you can turn a 2D drawing into a wearable costume. While a 2D drawing might look great on paper, it takes skill to create a costume that can move with you; this shows problem-solving skills.

Try to leave a lasting impression. The best way to do this is to be unique. If the hiring manager has seen the same Iron Man costume 20 times over the course of the con and you pop in wearing an Iron Man suit, you'll easily be forgettable. While I feel it is better to make something that will make you stand out, workshops always want and need technicians who can exactly replicate the required costume. If you want to showcase your ability to do so, just make sure you are the best Iron Man they see that day! Make sure all your surfaces are smooth and your paint job is perfect.

I cherish my job every day. I was super lucky to get an opportunity to work at Wētā Workshop thanks to the people I'd met through cosplay. I always tell people that it's not easy to get into Wētā Workshop, but it's even harder to stay there. I've been there for seven years now, and every week I stop and say to myself, "How good is this!" I am privileged to do what I love every day and to work with talented and passionate people. I get to learn from people with decades of experience

in the industry, and I don't take it for granted. I know that there are many who would love to do what I get to do, and I feel I owe it to them and to myself to give it my best every day.

If you aren't near a studio, make your own! While attending Fantasy Basel in 2018, I was talking to a cosplayer. He mentioned that he'd love to work on a movie one day but didn't know where to start as there were no local studios. After a few minutes, it hit me! We were talking right in front of the Swiss Cosplay Family booth. I asked him to turn around and look at his booth, and I told him the answer was right there. In the booth was a person working on leather armour, another was sewing, another was sculpting, and someone was painting their space gun. "There is your Wētā Workshop right there," I said. "If you all work together, you could make a short film for sure."

I truly believe that the cosplay community is filled with talented people and that working together we can create terrific projects. Over the last few years, I have seen amazing fan films popping up all over YouTube. The costumes, props, locations, acting, and special effects are all top-notch. This tells me that the maker community is working as it should—working together to enrich the world.

I'll finish off by saying that I believe the key to my success is hard work and the enjoyment of what I do. I hope this book will inspire you to think outside the norm and to start making costumes and props of your very own. Let your passion and creative mind guide you. Connect with other makers, and keep making our community positive and strong. You never know where it will take you.

ABOUT THE AUTHOR

SANIT KLAMCHANUAN is a Wellington-based artist, prop maker, and costumer who enjoys drawing and making cool stuff. Best known for adding his own design aesthetic to his costumes, he works at the world-renowned Weta Workshop, creating amazing costumes for well-known movies. Sanit travels the world to attend cosplay conventions, compete in, and judge contests.

COSPLAYER:
Spicythaidesign
COSTUME: Thai Armour,
original design

Photo by Sylvie Kirkman

FanPowered PRESS

Developed with our cosplay authors, FanPowered Press evokes how C&T's authors inspire and expand crafting topics by presenting innovative methods and ideas. We hope to inspire you to jump into something new and get outside of your comfort zone!

Want more creative content? Visit us online at **ctpub.com**